Michael

Faith and Philosophical Enquiry

Faith and Philosophical Enquiry

D. Z. PHILLIPS

London

Routledge & Kegan Paul

First published in 1970
by Routledge and Kegan Paul Limited
Broadway House, 68–74 Carter Lane,
London E.C.4.

Printed in Great Britain
The Camelot Press Ltd., London and Southampton
Set in 11 on 12 Baskerville

ISBN 0 7100 6847 6

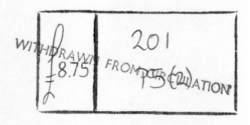

Contents

TO MY
MOTHER AND FATHER

Preface

Apart from inserting cross-references for the purposes of the present collection, the papers in this volume, for the most part, appear as originally published. The only exception worth mentioning is the second paper in the collection, 'Faith, Scepticism, and Religious Understanding'. Five paragraphs of the original have been omitted, since they were a quotation from the first paper included in the collection. Also, some slight, but important, changes have been made in the paper. These changes have been made in order to bring out the distinction between religious and philosophical understanding, a distinction which was unclear in the original version of the paper.

A word might be helpful about the order I have given to the papers. What I have tried to do is to begin the collection with six papers which I hope present the positive arguments I want to put forward in this collection. I think this is true of the fourth paper, even though it is a reply to the criticisms of philosophers. I am grateful to Professor J. R. Jones for permission to include our discussion as paper VI. The arguments of papers I–VI are involved in the reasons for the criticisms of some contemporary philosophers of religion in papers VII–IX. The implications of these arguments for more specific topics are investigated in papers X–XII. The final paper is a modest attempt at saying something about the character of philosophical enquiry, and of how important it is to realize this character in the philosophy of religion. It is an enquiry which might well take as its motto: 'Think not of Socrates, think of the truth'.

The original contexts in which the papers of this collection appeared are as follows: 'Philosophy, Theology and The Reality of God' (*The Philosophical Quarterly*, Vol. 13, 1963). 'Faith, Scepticism, and Religious Understanding' (*Religion and Understanding*, ed. D. Z. Phillips, Basil Blackwell, 1967). 'From World To God?' (*Proceedings of the Aristotelian Society*, Supp. Vol. LXI, 1967). 'Religious Belief and Philosophical Enquiry' (*Theology*, Vol. LXXI, No. 573, March 1968). 'Religious Beliefs and Language-Games' (*Ratio*, XII/I, 1970). 'Belief and Loss of Belief' (*Sophia*, 1970). 'Religion and Epistemology: some Contemporary Confusions' (*Australasian Journal of Philosophy*, 1966). 'Philosophy and Religious Education' (*British Journal of Educational Studies*, February 1970). 'Wisdom's Gods' (*The Philosophical Quarterly*, Vol. 19, 1969). 'Subjectivity and Religious Truth in Kierkegaard' (*Sophia*, 1968). 'God and Ought', 'On The Christian Concept of Love' (*Christian Ethics and Contemporary Philosophy*, ed. I. T. Ramsey, S.C.M. Press, 1966). 'Faith and Philosophy' (*Universities Quarterly*, March 1967).

I am grateful to all the editors and publishers concerned for permission to reprint the papers in this collection, and to Mr D. M. Evans for helping me with the proof reading.

D. Z. P.

Swansea

I Philosophy, Theology and the Reality of God

What kind of philosophical and theological account does the concept of divine reality call for? To answer this question one must determine the grammar of the concept to be investigated. All too often in the case of the reality of God this requirement has been overlooked or taken for granted. Because the question of divine reality can be construed as 'Is God real or not?' it has often been assumed that the dispute between the believer and the unbeliever is over *a matter of fact*. The philosophical investigation of the reality of God then becomes the philosophical investigation appropriate to an assertion of a matter of fact. That this is a misrepresentation of the religious concept is made obvious by a brief comparison of talk about facts with talk about God.

When do we say, 'It is a fact that...' or ask, 'Is it a fact that ...?'? Often, we do so where there is some uncertainty. For example, if the police hear that a wanted criminal has died in some remote part of the world, their reaction might be, 'Check the facts'. Again, we often say that something is a fact in order to rule out other possibilities. A student asks, 'Is the professor coming in today?' and receives the reply, 'No, as a matter of fact he never comes in on Monday.' A fact might not have been: it is conceivable that the wanted criminal had not died, just as it is conceivable that it had been the custom of the professor to come in on Mondays. On the other hand, the religious believer is not prepared to say that God might not exist. It is not that *as a matter of fact* God will always exist, but that it *makes no sense* to say that God might not exist.

We decide the truth or falsity of many matters of fact by taking account of the truth or falsity of other matters of fact. What is to count in deciding whether something is a fact or not is agreed upon in most cases. Refusal to admit that something is a fact in face of the maximum evidence might be cause for alarm, as in the case of someone who sees chairs in a room which in fact is empty. Is this akin to the dispute between the believer and the unbeliever; one sees God, but the other does not? The believer is not like someone who sees objects when they are not there, since his reaction to the absence of factual evidence is not at all like that of the man suffering from hallucinations. In the case of the chairs there is no dispute over *the kind of evidence* needed to settle the issue. When the positivist claims that there is no God because God cannot be located, the believer does not object on the grounds that the investigation has not been thorough enough, but on the grounds that the investigation fails to understand the grammar of what is being investigated – namely, the reality of God.

It makes as little sense to say, 'God's existence is not a fact' as it does to say, 'God's existence is a fact.' In saying that something either is or is not a fact, I am not describing the 'something' in question. To say that *x* is a fact is to say something about the grammar of *x*; it is to indicate what it would and would not be sensible to say or do in connection with it. To say that the concept of divine reality does not share this grammar is to reject the possibility of talking about God in the way in which one talks about matters of fact. I suggest that more can be gained if one compares the question, 'What kind of reality is divine reality?' not with the question, 'Is this physical object real or not?' but with the different question, 'What kind of reality is the reality of physical objects?'. To ask whether physical objects are real is not like asking whether this appearance is real or not where often one can find out. I can find out whether unicorns are real or not, but how can I find out whether the physical world is real or not? This latter question is not about the possibility of carrying out an investigation. It is a question of whether it is possible to speak of truth and falsity in the physical world; a question prior to that of determining the truth or falsity of any particular matter of fact. Similarly, the question of the reality of God is a question of the possibility of sense and nonsense, truth and falsity, in religion. When God's existence is construed as a matter of fact, it is taken for granted that the concept of God is at home within the conceptual framework of the reality of the physical world. It is as if we said, 'We know where the assertion of God's existence belongs, we understand what kind of assertion it is; all we need do is determine its truth or falsity.' But to ask a question about the reality of God is to ask a question about *a kind of reality*, not about the reality of *this* or *that*, in much the same way as asking a question about the reality of physical objects is not to ask about the reality of this or that physical object.

What then is the appropriate philosophical investigation of the reality of God? Suppose one asks, 'His reality as opposed to what?' The possibility of the unreality of

God does not occur *within* any religion, but it might well arise in disputes *between* religions. A believer of one religion might say that the believers of other religions were not worshipping the same God. The question how he would decide the identity of God is connected in many ways with what it means to talk of divine reality.

In a dispute over whether two people are discussing the same person there are ways of removing the doubt, but the identity of a god is not like the identity of a human being. To say that one worships the same God as someone else is not to point to the same object or to be confronted with it. How did Paul, for example, know that the God he worshipped was also the God of Abraham? What enabled him to say this was not anything like an objective method of agreement as in the case of two astronomers who check whether they are talking of the same star? What enabled Paul to say that he worshipped the God of Abraham was the fact that although many changes had taken place in the concept of God, there was nevertheless a common religious tradition in which both he and Abraham stood. To say that a god is not the same as one's own God involves saying that those who believe in him are in a radically different religious tradition from one's own. The criteria of what can sensibly be said of God are to be found *within* the religious tradition. This conclusion has an important bearing on the question of what account of religion philosophy and theology can give. It follows from my argument that the criteria of meaningfulness cannot be found *outside* religion, since they are given by religious discourse itself. Theology can claim justifiably to show what is meaningful in religion only when it has an internal relation to religious discourse. Philosophy

4

can make the same claim only if it is prepared to examine religious concepts in the contexts from which they derive their meaning.

Some theologians have claimed that theology gives a justification of religion. E. L. Mascall, for instance, says: 'The primary task of rational theology is to ask what grounds can be found for asserting the existence of God.'[1]*

Mascall implies that theology is external to religion and seeks a rational justification of religious truth. This view differs sharply from what I claim to be the internal role of theology in religion. This role can be explained as follows.

One cannot have religion without religious discourse. This is taught to children through stories by which they become acquainted with the attributes of God. As a result of this teaching the child forms an idea of God. We have far less idea than we sometimes suppose of what the nature of the child's idea is, but for our purposes its content is irrelevant. What is relevant to note is that the child does not listen to the stories, observe religious practices, reflect on all this, and then form an idea of God out of the experience. The idea of God is being formed in the actual story-telling and religious services. To ask which came first, the story-telling or the idea of God, is to ask a senseless question. Once one has an idea of God, what one has is a primitive theology. This is in many ways far removed from the theology of the professional theologian, but what makes it far removed is a difference in complexity or maturity, not a difference in kind or function. In each case theology

* All references appear at ends of chapters.

5

decides what it makes sense to say to God and about God. In short, theology is the grammar of religious discourse.

There is a limited analogy between the relation of theology to religious discourse and the relation of logic to language. One cannot have a language without a logic, although one can have a language without explicitly formulated logical principles. On the other hand, logical principles can have no meaning apart from the language in which they are found. This is not refuted by the fact that the meaning of a formal system can be explained in terms of the rules of that system. The question remains whether the possibility of any such system is dependent on the existence of language. The argument appears circular and contradictory if one thinks of either logic or language as being prior to the other. But as in the case of the child's stories and the concept of God, to ask which came first is to ask a senseless question. As soon as one has language one has logic which determines what can and what cannot be said in that language without being prior to it. As soon as one has religious discourse one has a theology which determines what it will be sensible to say and what it will be nonsensical to say within that religious discourse without being prior to it.

The limited nature of the analogy is evident when we want to talk of alternative theologies. To understand the need for a new theology, the need for a revised grammar of religious discourse, it is more helpful to consider an analogy with the development of scientific laws. In the course of scientific experimentation, in order to account for new phenomena, scientific laws have to be modified or changed. One would not say

6

that the old laws are wrong, or that the new ones are nearer the truth, but simply that they differ in their range of application. There is an analogy here with the way in which old ideas of God are supplanted and new ones take their place. This will not seem arbitrary if one remembers that the need for a new theology, for a different idea of God, does not occur *in vacuo*. The development of scientific laws can only be understood by reference to the tradition of scientific enquiry, and the changes in the idea of God can only be understood in terms of a developing religion. This is not to say that the role of the concept of God is akin to the role of a scientific model, for the analogy with developing scientific laws, like the analogy with logic and language, is a limited one. I use it simply to re-emphasize the internal relation of theology to religion.

Theology cannot impose criteria of meaningfulness on religion from without. Neither can philosophy. Mascall, on the other hand, maintains that like theology, philosophy has a special role to play, namely to seek rational grounds for asserting the existence of God. This view misrepresents the relation of philosophy to religion. The role of philosophy in this context is not to justify, but to understand. Mascall says of the Christian: 'He knows what he means by God because the Bible and the Church have told him. He can then institute a purely rational enquiry into the grounds for asserting that God exists.'[2]

Why not remain with an understanding of what the Bible and the Church teach? What extra is this rational enquiry supposed to achieve? This question might be answered by indicating the problems connected with the existence of a plurality of religions. If one accepts the internal relation of theology to religion and the religious tradition as the means of identifying God, what is one to say of the conflicting claims of different religions? In much the same spirit in which I have been talking about the relation of theology to religion, Peter Winch says:

> . . . criteria of logic are not a direct gift of God, but arise out of, and are only intelligible in the context of, ways of living or modes of social life. It follows that one cannot apply criteria of logic to modes of social life as such. For instance, science is one such mode and religion is another; and each has criteria of intelligibility peculiar to itself. So within science or religion actions can be logical or illogical . . . in religion it would be illogical to suppose that one could pit one's strength against God's . . . But we cannot sensibly say that either the practice of science itself or that of religion is either illogical or logical; both are non-logical.[3]

But can this thesis hold in face of a plurality of religions? The problem is brought out if one considers the way in which the analogy between theology, logic and scientific laws which we have considered breaks down. In the development of scientific laws there is eventual agreement that such development is desirable. The same could be said, roughly speaking, of the development of the idea of God in the Old Testament. But this need not be true of modern developments in theology: opposing theologians will stick to their respective positions and declare the others to be wrong. This brings up the question of authority or reference to an authoritative system. Both logic and science are *public* in so far as it can be decided whether a statement is logical or illogical, or whether a given practice is scientific or not. Illogical and non-scientific statements are refutable. But because of the nature of theology one may only say that a religious statement is refuted by *a* theology. There is no analogy here with either logic or science. This is due to what might be called *the personal element* in theology. In the formulation of logical and scientific principles there is no personal element involved. This is not true of theology.

As I have already said, the systematic theology is a sophistication of that theology which is necessarily present in so far as religious language is present. The theological system is often constructed to answer certain questions and problems which may arise. But the foundation of a theological system is based on the non-formalized theology which is within the religious way of life carried on by the person who is constructing the theological system. In so far as this is true, theology is personal, since it is based on one's own experience of God. Where the connection between theology and experience is missing, there is a danger of theology becoming an academic game.

It is extremely difficult to steer a course between the personal and the public in this whole question. Theology must be personal in so far as it is concerned with one's own idea of God, and in this context religion must always be personal. On the other hand, in so far as religious language must be learnt, religion is public. One cannot have *any* idea of God. Once one has embraced a theology, one has established 'what can be said' in that particular religion, but what can be said does not depend on the fact that an *individual* is saying it.

Some philosophers have held that in face of theological differences *within* religions and the more pronounced theological differences *between* religions, philosophy itself must decide what are the meaningful religious assertions. This view is expressed in no uncertain terms by Peter Munz in his book, *Problems of Religious Knowledge*. In face of the plurality of religious traditions Munz thinks it foolish to identify the truth with any *one* of them. On the other hand, he also objects to saying that religious truth is *the sum* of religious traditions. One of Munz's aims is '. . . to enquire whether it is not possible to find a criterion of religious truth which would enable us to avoid the identification of religious truth with any one provincial or with the alleged cosmopolitan tradition.'[4]

Munz thinks that such a criterion can be found in philosophy: '. . . the philosophy of religion imposes its own criterion of what is good theological reasoning and what is bad theological reasoning. And in doing this, it ceases to be purely descriptive of religious knowledge and begins to be normative.'[5]

Munz's disagreement with Winch is obvious. He thinks that the norm of truth and falsity is not to be found within religion, but *outside* it. One reason why he thinks that philosophical criteria of theological reasoning are needed is the absence of real discussion between adherents of different religions. He describes the contact that does occur as follows: 'These arguments are therefore no more than affirmations of positions. They are monologues. A real argument must be a dialogue, an exchange of opinions and a weighing of evidence. Only a *real* argument can be more than an exercise in self-assertion. But to argue *really*, one must be clear as to the things one is arguing about.'[6]

Munz says more than he realizes in the last sentence of the above quotation. In order for adherents of different religions to talk to each other, they must have something to talk about! But this is a religious matter, not a philosophical one. Philosophical speculation may help to distinguish religion from superstition, but where *religions* are concerned, whether they have enough in common to promote discussion depends on the content of their beliefs. No general answer is possible. In some cases, for instance between Christians and Jews, a wealth of discussion is possible. Between others – Christians and Buddhists, say – discussion is more difficult. When one considers tribal religions, one wonders whether one is talking about the same thing at all; whether here religion has a different meaning. The possibility of discussion then depends, not as Munz suggests on the intervention of philosophy from without, but on the theologies of the religions in question. If there were a union of religions this would be because of changes within the religions united. One might object to my analysis on the grounds that it stresses religious meaning at the expense of religious truth. The analysis does not indicate which religion is the true one. But why should anyone suppose that philosophy can answer that question?

One final objection. An opponent of religion might claim that far from leaving the question of religious truth unanswered, I have guaranteed that any possible answer is favourable to religion by insisting that the criteria of intelligibility in religious matters are to be

11

found within religion. The objection confuses my epistemological thesis with an absurd religious doctrine. To say that the criteria of truth and falsity in religion are to be found within a religious tradition is to say nothing of the truth or falsity of the religion in question. On the contrary, my thesis is as necessary in explaining unbelief as it is in explaining belief. It is because many have seen religion for what it is that they have thought it important to rebel against it. The rebel sees what religion is and rejects it. What can this 'seeing' be? Obviously, he does not see the point of religion as the believer does, since for the believer seeing the point of religion is believing. Nevertheless, the rebel has knelt in the church even if he has not prayed. He has taken the sacrament of Communion even if he has not communed. He knows the story from the inside, but it is not a story that captivates him. Nevertheless, he can see what religion is supposed to do and what it is supposed to be. At times we stand afar off saying, 'I wish I could be like that.' We are not like that, but we know what it must be like. The rebel stands on the threshold of religion seeing what it must be like, but saying, 'I do not want to be like that. I rebel against it all.' It is in this context, as Camus has said, that 'every blasphemy is, ultimately, a participation in holiness'.

References

1. *Existence and Analogy*, 1.
2. *Ibid.*, 17.
3. *The Idea of a Social Science*, 90–1.
4. *Problems of Religious Knowledge*, 9.
5. *Ibid.*, 28.
6. *Ibid.*, 11.

II Faith, Scepticism, and Religious Understanding

The relation between religion and philosophical reflection needs to be reconsidered. For the most part, in recent philosophy of religion, philosophers, believers, and non-believers alike, have been concerned with discovering *the grounds* of religious belief. Philosophy, they claim, is concerned with reasons; it considers what is to count as good evidence for a belief. In the case of religious beliefs, the philosopher ought to enquire into the reasons anyone could have for believing in the existence of God, for believing that life is a gift from God, or for believing that an action is the will of God. Where can such reasons be found? One class of reasons comes readily to mind. Religious believers, when asked why they believe in God, may reply in a variety of ways. They may say, 'I have had an experience of the living God', 'I believe on the Lord Jesus Christ', 'God saved me while I was a sinner', or, 'I just can't help believing'. Philosophers have not given such reasons very much attention. The so-called trouble is not so much with the content of the replies as with the fact that the replies are made by believers. The answers come from *within* religion, they presuppose the framework of Faith, and therefore cannot be treated as *evidence* for religious belief. Many philosophers who argue in this way seem to be

13

searching for evidence or reasons for religious beliefs *external* to belief itself. It is assumed that such evidence and reasons would, if found, constitute the grounds of religious belief.

The philosophical assumption behind the ignoring of religious testimony as begging the question, and the search for external reasons for believing in God, is that one could settle the question of whether there is a God or not without referring to the form of life of which belief in God is a fundamental part. What would it be like for a philosopher to settle the question of the existence of God? Could a philosopher say that he believed that God exists and yet never pray to Him, rebel against Him, lament the fact that he could no longer pray, aspire to deepen his devotion, seek His will, try to hide from Him, or fear and tremble before Him? In short, could a man believe that God exists without his life being touched *at all* by the belief? Norman Malcolm asks with good reason, 'Would a belief that he exists, if it were completely non-affective, really be a belief that he exists? Would it be anything at all? What is "the form of life" into which it would enter? What difference would it make whether anyone did or did not have this belief?'[1]

Yet many philosophers who search for the grounds of religious belief, claim, to their own satisfaction at least, to understand what a purely theoretical belief in the existence of God would be. But the accounts these philosophers give of what religious believers seem to be saying are often at variance with what many believers say, at least, when *they* are not philosophizing. Every student of the philosophy of religion will have been struck by the amount of talking at cross purposes within the subject. A philosopher may say that there is no God, but a believer may reply, 'You are creating and then attacking a fiction. The god whose existence you deny is not the God I believe in.' Another philosopher may say that religion is meaningless, but another believer may reply, 'You say that when applied to God, words such as "exists", "love", "will", etc., do not mean what they signify in certain non-religious contexts. I agree. You conclude from this that religion is meaningless, whereas the truth is that you are failing to grasp the meaning religion has.' Why is there this lack of contact between many philosophers and religious believers? One reason is that many philosophers who do not believe that God exists assume that they know what it means to say that there is a God. Norman Kemp Smith made a penetrating analysis of this fact when commenting on the widespread belief among American philosophers in his day of the uselessness of philosophy of religion.

. . . those who are of this way of thinking, however they may have thrown over the religious beliefs of the communities in which they have been nurtured, still continue to be influenced by the phraseology of religious devotion – a phraseology which, in its endeavour to be concrete and universally intelligible, is at little pains to guard against the misunderstandings to which it may so easily give rise. As they insist upon, and even exaggerate, the merely literal meaning of this phraseology, the God in whom they have ceased to believe is a Being whom they picture in an utterly anthropomorphic fashion. . . .[2]

The distinction between religious believers and atheistical philosophers is not, of course, as clear-cut as I have suggested. It is all too evident in contemporary philosophy of religion that many philosophers who *do* believe in God philosophize about religion in the way which Kemp Smith found to be true of philosophical non-believers. Here, one can say either that their philosophy reflects their belief, in which case they believe in superstition but not in God, or, taking the more charitable view, that they are failing to give a good philosophical account of what they really believe.

Insufficient attention has been paid to the question of what kind of philosophical enquiry the concept of divine reality calls for. Many philosophers assume that everyone knows *what* it means to say that there is a God, and that the only outstanding question is *whether* there is a God. Similarly, it might be thought, everyone knows what it means to say that there are unicorns, although people may disagree over whether in fact there are any unicorns. If there were an analogy between the existence of God and the existence of unicorns, then coming to see that there is a God would be like coming to see that an additional being exists. 'I know what people are doing when they worship,' a philosopher might say. 'They praise, they confess, they thank, and they ask for things. The only difference between myself and religious believers is that I do not believe that there is a being who receives their worship.' The assumption, here, is that the meaning of worship is contingently related to the question whether there is a God or not. The assumption might be justified by saying that there need be no consequences of existential beliefs. Just as one can say, 'There is a planet Mars, but I couldn't care less,' so one can say, 'There is a God, but I couldn't care less.' But what is one *saying* here when one says that there is a God? Despite the fact that one need take no interest in the existence of a planet, an account could be given of the kind of difference the existence of the planet makes, and of how one could find out whether the planet exists or not. But all this is foreign to the question whether there is a God. That is not something anyone could *find out*. It has been far too readily assumed that the dispute between the believer and the unbeliever is over a *matter of fact*. Philosophical reflection on the reality of God then becomes the philosophical reflection appropriate to an assertion of a matter of fact. I have tried to show that this is a misrepresentation of the religious concept, and that philosophy can claim justifiably to show what is meaningful in religion only if it is prepared to examine religious concepts in the contexts from which they derive their meaning.[3]

A failure to take account of the above context has led some philosophers to ask religious language to satisfy criteria of meaningfulness alien to it. They say that religion must be rational if it is to be intelligible. Certainly, the distinction between the rational and the irrational must be central in any account one gives of meaning. But this is not to say that there is a paradigm of rationality to which all modes of discourse conform. A necessary prolegomenon to the philosophy of religion, then, is to show the diversity of criteria of rationality; to show that the distinction between the real and the unreal does not come to the same thing in every context. If this were observed, one would no longer wish to construe God's reality as being that of an existent among existents, an object among objects.

Coming to see that there is a God is not like coming to see that an additional being exists. If it were, there would be an extension of one's knowledge of facts, but no extension of one's understanding. Coming to see that there is a God involves seeing a new meaning in one's life, and being given a new understanding. The Hebrew-Christian conception of God is not a conception of a being among beings. Kierkegaard emphasized the point when he said bluntly, 'God does not exist. He is eternal.'[4]

The distinction between eternity and existence has been ignored by many philosophers of religion, and as a result they have singled out particular religious beliefs for discussion, divorcing them from the context of belief in God. Alasdair MacIntyre has pointed out the importance of recognizing the need, not simply to discuss specific religious utterances, but to ask why such utterances are called religious in the first place.

> Those linguistic analysts who have turned their attention to theology have begun to examine in detail particular religious utterances and theological concepts. This examination of the logic of religious language has gone with a great variety of religious attitudes on the part of the philosophers concerned. Some have been sceptics, others believers. But what their enterprise has had in common is an examination of *particular* religious forms of speech and utterance, whether such examination has been presented as part of an argument for or as part of an argument against belief. What such examinations may omit is a general consideration of what it means to call a particular assertion or utterance part of a religious belief as distinct from a moral code or a scientific theory.[5]

In his more recent work in the philosophy of religion, MacIntyre has said that the above distinction buys a position at the price of emptiness,[6] but I think his earlier view is the correct one. It stresses the artificiality of separating the love, mercy, or forgiveness of God from His nature. One cannot understand what praising, confessing, thanking, or asking mean in worship apart from belief in an eternal God. The eternity of the Being addressed determines the meaning of all these activities. One implication of this fact is that philosophers who do not see anything in belief in God can no longer think of their rejection as the denial of something *with which they are familiar*. Discovering that belief in God is meaningful is not like establishing that something is the case within a universe of discourse with which we are already familiar. On the contrary, it is to discover that there *is* a universe of discourse we had been unaware of. The flattering picture that the academic philosopher may have of himself as possessing the key to reality has to be abandoned. The philosopher, like anyone else, may fail to understand what it means to believe in an eternal God.

In saying that one must take account of the concept of the eternal if one wishes to understand various religious activities, I realize that I am laying myself open to all kinds of misunderstandings. Some religious believers, when they have wanted to turn aside the philosopher's questions, have said, 'Finite understanding cannot understand the eternal,' or something similar. This is not what I am saying. There is a proper place to say such things, that God is the inexpressible, for example, but that place is within religious belief. These are religious utterances whose meaning is seen in the role they play in the lives of believers. Sometimes, however, the utterances are used as a form of protectionism against intellectual enquiry. They began as religious utterances, but end up as pseudo-epistemological theories.[7] When this happens, the philosopher's censure is deserved. In saying that human understanding cannot fathom the eternal, the believer is claiming that there is some higher order of things that transcends all human discourse, that religion expresses 'the nature of things'. In saying this, the believer falsifies the facts. Such a position involves upholding what John Anderson calls 'a hierarchical doctrine of reality'. Anderson has a powerful argument against this brand of religious apologetics. He says that to speak in this way

> . . . is to speak on behalf of the principle of authority – and so again (whatever the actual power may be that is thus metaphysically bolstered up) to support a low way of living. It is low, in particular, because it is anti-intellectual, because it is necessarily dogmatic. Some account can be given of the relation of a particular 'rule' or way of behaving to a certain way of life, but it can have no demonstrable relation to 'the nature of things'. To say that something is required by the nature of things is just to say that it is required – to say, without reason, that it 'is to be done'; and, as soon as any specification is attempted, the whole structure breaks down. If, for example, we are told to do something because God commands us to do so, we can immediately ask why we should do what God commands – and any intelligible answer brings us back to *human* relationships, to the struggle between opposing movements.[8]

I should like to make it quite clear that I agree with Anderson in the above criticism. In speaking of religion as turning away from the temporal towards the eternal, I am not putting forward any kind of epistemological thesis. On the contrary, I am referring to the way in which the concept of the eternal does play a role in very many human relationships. I am anxious to show that religion is not some kind of technical discourse or esoteric pursuit cut off from the ordinary problems and perplexities, hopes, and joys which most of us experience at some time or other. If it were, it would not have the importance it does have for so many people. By considering one example in detail – namely, eternal love or the love of God – I shall try to show what significance it has in human experience, the kind of circumstances which occasion it, and the kind of human predicament it answers. By so doing I hope to illustrate how seeing that there is a God in this context is synonymous with seeing the possibility of eternal love.[9]

Let me begin by speaking of a distinction with which we are all familiar: the distinction between *mine* and *yours*. The distinction is relevant to the concept of justice. If I take what is yours, or if you take what is mine, justice is thereby transgressed against. Our relationships with other people are pervaded by a wide range of rights and obligations, many of which serve to emphasize the distinction between *mine* and *yours*. But all human relationships are not like this. In erotic love and in friendship, the distinction between *mine* and *yours* is broken down. The lovers or the friends may say, 'All I have is his, and what is his is mine.' Kierkegaard says that the distinction between *mine* and *yours* has been transformed by a relationship in which the key term is *ours*. Nevertheless, he goes on to show that the *mine/yours* distinction is not completely transformed by such relationships, since the *ours* now functions as a new *mine* for the partners in the relationships. The distinguishing factor in the *mine/yours* distinction is now the relation of erotic love or friendship as opposed to the self-love which prevailed previously. *Mine* and *yours* now refer to those who are within and to those who are outside the specific relationship.

Now, Christianity wishes to speak of a kind of love which is such that no man is excluded from it. It calls this love 'love of one's neighbour'. What is more, it claims that this love is internally related to the love of God; that is, that without knowing what this love is, one cannot know what the love of God is either. An attempt to elucidate what is meant by love of the neighbour will therefore be an attempt to elucidate what is meant by the love of God.

If one considers self-love in its simplest form – namely, as the desire to possess the maximum of what one considers to be good for oneself – it is easy enough to imagine conditions in which such love could be thwarted. War, famine, or some other natural disaster might upset the normal conditions in which rights and obligations operate. Even given such conditions, the self-lover's ambitions may be thwarted by the greater ingenuity of his competitors. Sooner or later he may be forced to realize that the minimum rather than the maximum is going to be his lot. Self-love might be called temporal love in so far as it depends on states of affairs contingently related to itself. If a man's life revolves around self-love, it is obvious that he is forever dependent on the way things go, since it is the way things go that determines whether his self-love is satisfied or not.

It might be thought that erotic love and friendship avoid the predicament of self-love outlined above. The lovers or the friends may say to one another, 'Come what may, we still have each other.' Yet, such reliance shows that this love too is temporal; it depends on certain states of affairs being realized. To begin with, the point of such love depends on the existence of *the other*. Often, when the lovers or the friends love each other very much, the death of the beloved can rob life of its meaning; for what is love without the beloved? Again, erotic love and friendship depend on the unchangeability of the beloved. But the beloved may change. Friendship can cool, and love can fade. If the relationship is such that it depended on reciprocation, then a change in the beloved or in the friend may rob it of its point. So although erotic love and friendship are far removed from self-love, they too are forms of temporal love in so far as they are dependent on how things go.

Temporal love, then, is marked by certain characteristics: it depends on how things go, it may change, and it may end in failure. Eternal love, it is said, is not dependent on how things go, it cannot change, and it cannot suffer defeat. One must not think that this contrast presents the believer with an either/or. He is not asked to choose between loving God on the one hand and loving the loved one on the other. What he is asked to do is not to love the loved one in such a way that the love of God becomes impossible. The death of the beloved must not rob life of its meaning, since for the believer the meaning of life is found in God. The believer claims that there is a love that will not let one go whatever happens. This is the love of God, the independence of which from what happens is

23

closely bound up with the point of calling it eternal.

The object of Christian love is the neighbour. But who is the neighbour? The neighbour is every man. The obligation to love the neighbour does not depend on the particularity of the relationship, as in the case of the love which exists between parents and children, lovers or friends. The neighbour is not loved because of his being a parent, lover, or friend, but simply because of his being. In relation to the agent, the love takes the form of self-renunciation. In this self-renunciation, man discovers the Spirit of God. Consider how love of the neighbour exhibits the three characteristics I mentioned earlier: independence of the way things go, unchangeability, and immunity from defeat. Kierkegaard brings out the contrast between love of one's neighbour on the one hand, and erotic love and friendship on the other, in these terms.

> The beloved can treat you in such a way that he is lost to you, and you can lose a friend, but whatever a neighbour does to you, you can never lose him. To be sure, you can also continue to love your beloved and your friend no matter how they treat you, but you cannot truthfully continue to call them beloved and friend when they, sorry to say, have really changed. No change, however, can take your neighbour from you, for it is not your neighbour who holds you fast – it is your love which holds your neighbour fast.[10]

For someone with eyes only for the prudential, and common-sense considerations, the love which Kierkegaard is talking about seems to lead inevitably to self-deception, and to a kind of foolishness. On the contrary, Kierkegaard argues, eternal love is precisely the only kind of love which can never deceive one. After a certain stage of unrequited love, no one could be blamed for saying, 'The lover has deceived me.' It becomes intelligible and justifiable to say this because the love in question does not have much point without some degree of reciprocation. At first sight it looks as if the same conclusions apply to love of one's neighbour. But eternal love believes all things, and yet is never deceived! Ordinarily speaking, we say that only a fool believes all things; only a man who ignores the odds could be so stupid. Yet, Christianity says that eternal love cannot be deceived, for if a believer is wrong about a man but continues to love him, in what sense is he deceived? True, one can enumerate all the ways in which obvious deceptions have taken place: loans unreturned, promises broken, trusts betrayed, etc., but the believer continues to love the neighbour despite all this. Those who see little in the love of the neighbour will say, especially if the believer is reduced to a state which many would call ruin, that the believer has lost all. On the contrary, Kierkegaard tells us, the believer, in the act of self-renunciation, possesses all; he possesses love. To possess this love is to possess God. Indeed, the only way in which the believer can be deceived is by ceasing to love. Ordinarily, when we say, 'I shall show no more love towards him,' we envisage the loss as suffered by the person who is the object of one's love. But if the believer says, 'I shall love the neighbour no longer,' he is the victim of deception, since the loss of loving is his loss too. Kierkegaard brings this point out very clearly:

When someone says, 'I have given up my love for this man,' he thinks that it is this person who loses,

this person who was the object of his love. The speaker
thinks that he himself possesses his love in the same
sense as when one who has supported another
financially says, 'I have quit giving assistance to him.'
In this case the giver keeps for himself the money
which the other previously received, he who is the
loser, for the giver is certainly far from losing by this
financial shift. But it is not like this with love; perhaps
the one who was the object of love does lose, but he
who 'has given up his love for this man' is the loser.
Maybe he does not detect this himself; perhaps he
does not detect that the language mocks him, for he
says explicitly, 'I have given up my love.' But if he
has given up his love, he has then ceased to be loving.
True enough, he adds 'my love for this man', but
this does not help when love is involved, although in
money matters one can manage things this way without loss to oneself. The adjective *loving* does not apply
to me when I have given up my love 'for this man' –
alas, even though I perhaps imagined that he was
the one who lost. It is the same with despairing over
another person; it is oneself who is in despair.[11]

In this way, Kierkegaard illustrates the truth that for
the believer, love itself is the real object of the relationship between himself and another person. This love is
the Spirit of God, and to possess it is to walk with God.
Once this is realized, one can see how love and understanding are equated in Christianity. To know God is to
love Him. There is no theoretical understanding of the
reality of God.

If anyone thinks he is a Christian and yet is indifferent
towards his being a Christian, then he really is not

one at all. What would we think of a man who affirmed that he was in love and also that it was a matter of indifference to him?[12]

'But, so far,' the non-believer might complain, 'you have simply concealed the advantage entailed in religion, namely, God's love for the sinner. Is not this the reason for love of the neighbour? Unless one loves the neighbour, God will not love one.' There is truth in this *unless*, but not as conceived in the above objection. The love of the neighbour is not the means whereby a further end is realized – namely, one's own forgiveness. On the contrary, there is an internal relation between forgiving another and being forgiven oneself. I cannot hope to emulate Kierkegaard's analysis of this religious truth, so I must ask the reader to forgive a final quotation of two passages where his analysis is particularly forceful:

When we say, 'Love saves from death,' there is straightway a reduplication in thought: the lover saves another human being from death, and in entirely the same or yet in a different sense he saves himself from death. This he does at the same time; it is one and the same; he does not save the other at one moment and at another save himself, but in the moment he saves the other he saves himself from death. Only love never thinks about the latter, about saving oneself, about acquiring confidence itself; the lover in love thinks only about giving confidence and saving another from death. But the lover is not thereby forgotten. No, he who in love forgets himself, forgets his sufferings in order to think of another's, forgets all his wretchedness in order to think of another's,

forgets what he himself loses in order lovingly to consider another's loss, forgets his advantage in order
lovingly to look after another's advantage: truly, such
a person is not forgotten. There is one who thinks of
him, God in heaven; or love thinks of him. God is
love, and when a human being because of love forgets
himself, how then should God forget him! No, while
the lover forgets himself and thinks of the other
person, God thinks of the lover. The self-lover is busy;
he shouts and complains and insists on his rights in
order to make sure he is not forgotten – and yet he is
forgotten. But the lover, who forgets himself, is
remembered by love. There is one who thinks of him,
and in this way it comes about that the lover gets
what he gives.[13]

And again:

'*Forgive, and you will also be forgiven.*' Meanwhile, one
might nevertheless manage to understand these words
in such a way that he imagined it possible to receive
forgiveness without his forgiving. Truly this is a misunderstanding. Christianity's view is: forgiveness *is*
forgiveness: your forgiveness is your forgiveness;
your forgiveness of another is your own forgiveness: the
forgiveness which you give you receive, not contrari-
wise that you give the forgiveness which you receive.
It is as if Christianity would say: pray to God humbly
and believing in your forgiveness, for he really is
compassionate in such a way as no human being is;
but if you will test how it is with respect to the forgiveness, then observe yourself. If honestly before
God you wholeheartedly forgive your enemy (but
remember that if you do, God sees it), then you dare

hope also for your forgiveness, for it is one and the same. God forgives you neither more nor less nor otherwise than *as* you forgive your trespassers. It is only an illusion to imagine that one himself has forgiveness, although one is slack in forgiving others.[14]

My purpose in discussing the Christian concept of love was to show how coming to see the possibility of such love amounts to the same thing as coming to see the possibility of belief in God. As I said earlier, to know God is to love Him, and the understanding which such knowledge brings is the understanding of love. Belief, understanding, and love can all be equated with each other in this context. There are, however, certain objections which can be made against this conclusion. Before ending, I want to consider one of the strongest of these made recently by Alasdair MacIntyre:

> And if the believer wishes to he can always claim that we can only disagree with him because we do not understand him. But the implications of this defence of belief are more fatal to it than any attack could be.[15]

One of the fatal implications of identifying understanding and believing, according to MacIntyre, is that one can no longer give an intelligible account of a rejection of religious belief. MacIntyre says that the Protestant who claims that grace is necessary before one can possess religious understanding is soon convicted of paradox.

> For the Protestant will elsewhere deny what is entailed by his position, namely that nobody ever rejects Christianity (since anyone who thinks he has

29

rejected it must have lacked saving grace and so did not understand Christianity and so in fact rejected something else).[16]

Does MacIntyre's point hold for any identification of understanding and believing? I suggest not. To begin with, there is a perfectly natural use of the word *rejection* which is connected with the inability of the person who rejects to make any sense of what is rejected. I can see no objection to saying that the man who says that religion means nothing to him rejects the claims of religion on his life. Apparently, when Oscar Wilde was accused of blasphemy during his trial, he replied 'Sir, blasphemy is a word I never use.' Wilde is rejecting a certain way of talking. Similarly, the man who says, 'Religion is mumbo-jumbo as far as I am concerned,' is making a wholesale rejection of a way of talking or a way of life. That way of talking and that way of life mean nothing to him, but this does not mean that he cannot reject them.

On the other hand, I agree with MacIntyre that there are difficulties involved in the view I wish to maintain if the rejection of religion in question is not the rejection of the meaningless, but rebellion against God. Camus says of the rebel:

> The rebel defies more than he denies. Originally, at least, he does not deny God, he simply talks to Him as an equal. But it is not a polite dialogue. It is a polemic animated by the desire to conquer.[17]

But if the rebel knows God and yet defies Him, how can one say that to know God is to love Him? Clearly, some kind of modification of my thesis is called for. I agree. But what is not called for is a denial of the identification of belief and understanding in religion. The fact of rebellion makes one think otherwise because of a false and unnecessary assimilation of 'I believe in God' to 'I believe in John'. Belief in God has a wider range of application than belief in another person. This point has been made very clearly by Norman Malcolm:

> Belief in a person primarily connotes trust or faith: but this is not so of belief in God. A man could properly be said to believe in God whose chief attitude towards God was *fear*. ('A sword is sent upon you, and who may turn it back?') But if you were enormously afraid of another human being you could not be said to believe in him. At least you would not believe in him *in so far* as you were afraid of him: whereas the fear of God is one form of belief in Him.
>
> I am suggesting that *belief-in* has a wider meaning when God is the object of it than when a human being is. Belief in God encompasses not only trust but also awe, dread, dismay, resentment, and perhaps even hatred. Belief in God will involve some affective state or attitude, having God as its object, and those attitudes could vary from reverential love to rebellious rejection.[18]

I should still want to argue, however, that the love of God is the primary form of belief in God if only because the intelligibility of all the other attitudes Malcolm mentions is logically dependent on it. The rebel must see the kind of relationship God asks of the believer before he can reject and defy it. He sees the story from the inside, but it is not a story that captivates him. The love of God is active in his life, but in him it evokes hatred. To say that he does not believe in God is absurd, for whom does he hate if not God?

Similar difficulties to those mentioned by MacIntyre might be thought to arise in giving an account of seeking for God. If one must believe before one can know God, how can one know that it is God one is seeking for? The answer to this difficulty has been given by Pascal: 'Comfort yourself, you would not seek me if you had not found me.' One must not think of belief in God as an all-or-nothing affair. Whether the love of God means anything in a man's life can be assessed, not simply by his attainments, but also by his aspirations. So even if a man does not actually love God, his understanding of what it means to love God can be shown by his aspirations towards such love.

On the other hand, it would be a mistake to conclude that in the absence of religious attainments only religious aspirations could be the sign that religion held some meaning for a person. We have seen already in the case of the rebel that belief in God need not entail a worshipful attitude on the part of the believer. Neither need the believer aspire to attain love of God. On the contrary, he may want to flee from it. Instead of feeling sad because he spurns God's love, he may hate the fact that he cannot rid his life of God. If someone were to say to him, 'You do not believe in God', he might reply, 'How can you say that when God will not leave me alone?'

What, then, are our conclusions? The assertion that to know God is to love Him is false if it is taken to imply that everyone who believes in God loves Him. What it stresses, quite correctly, is that there is no theoretical knowledge of God. As Malcolm said, 'belief in God involves some affective state or attitude'. I think that

Faith, Scepticism, and Religious Understanding

love of God is fundamental in religion, since all other attitudes can be explained by reference to it. I believe that Kierkegaard says somewhere that in relation to God there are only lovers – happy or unhappy – but lovers. The unhappy or unruly lover has an understanding of what it means to believe in God as well as the happy lover. The man who construes religious belief as a theoretical affair distorts it. Kierkegaard emphasizes that there is no understanding of religion without passion. And when the philosopher understands that, *his* understanding of religion is incompatible with scepticism.

References

1. 'Is it a Religious Belief that "God Exists"?' in *Faith and the Philosophers*, ed. John Hick, London, 1964, 107.
2. 'Is Divine Existence Credible?' in *Religion and Understanding*, ed. D. Z. Phillips, Blackwell, 1967, 105–6.
3. See pages 1–5 of the previous chapter.
4. *Concluding Unscientific Postscript*, 296.
5. 'The Logical Status of Religious Belief', in *Metaphysical Beliefs*, ed. A. MacIntyre, London, 1957, 172.
6. See 'Is Understanding Religion Compatible with Believing?' in *Faith and the Philosophers*, ed. John Hick, London, 1964.
7. See ch. V.
8. 'Art and Morality', *Australasian Journal of Psychology and Philosophy*, XIX (December, 1941), 256–7.
9. Anyone acquainted with Kierkegaard's *Works of Love* will recognize in what follows how dependent I am on the second part of that work.
10. *Op. cit.*, 76.

11. *Ibid.*, 239–40.
12. *Ibid.*, 42.
13. *Ibid.*, 262.
14. *Ibid.*, 351–2.
15. 'Is Understanding Religion Compatible with Believing?', *Faith and the Philosophers*, 133.
16. *Ibid.*, 116.
17. *The Rebel*, Peregrine Book edn., trans. by Anthony Bower, 31.
18. *Op. cit.*, 106–7.

III From World to God?

The publication of Norman Malcolm's paper on 'Anselm's Ontological Arguments' led to a revival of interest in these traditional arguments for the existence of God.[1] There has been no comparable revival of interest in cosmological arguments which seek to establish the same conclusion. Part of the reason for this, perhaps, is that the way in which Anselm's arguments are reconsidered does not go against the current anti-metaphysical character of philosophical enquiry. Despite many opinions to the contrary, it cannot be said that Malcolm argues from the logical possibility of concepts to the real possibility of things. What he is concerned to show, and what he believes Anselm is concerned to show, is that real possibilities are not exhausted by the real possibility of things. God is not a thing; He is not an existent among existents. What is important to note for our purposes, however, is that Malcolm does not reach these conclusions by means of metaphysical arguments. He claims to have done so by examining, within the Hebrew and Christian traditions, what worship of an eternal God means to those who practise it. St Anselm states in the Preface to his *Proslogion*, 'I have written the following treatise in the person of one who . . . seeks to understand what he believes'. But how can religious beliefs which are not based on philosophical arguments, nevertheless, be understood better by means of such arguments? John Baillie suggests that

> The only possible answer would be to claim that the argument which was afterwards hit upon was no more than the clear explication of a logical structure which had been already 'implicitly' contained in the mental process by which the faith was originally acquired; and though St Anselm never explains himself on this point, it would appear that something of the sort was in his mind:[2]

Whatever Anselm had in mind, it is clear that Malcolm sees one of the main contributions of the ontological argument to be a clarification of the grammar of the reality of God in Hebrew and Christian traditions. To some extent, an atheist can grasp these points of logical grammar, and, while remaining an atheist, assent to the ontological argument.

When we consider cosmological arguments for the existence of God, the position seems radically different. Here, there seems to be no suggestion that the proof is simply the explication of the logic of religious beliefs held independently of it. It is claimed that the existence of God can be demonstrated from the existence of the world. The arguments seek a transcendental explanation: they are an attempt to explain the world, to account for its existence, in terms of something other than the world – namely, God. The ultimate explanation of the world can be arrived at by reason alone without the aid of revealed truths. On the other hand, the God whose existence is 'proved' by the arguments is said to be *the same* God as the God known through faith. It is unclear how this judgment of identity is to be made.

What is clear is that this identity is often taken for granted. For example, it has been said that Aquinas had a distaste for philosophical-sounding arguments, and took as his starting-point 'a notion more familiar to ordinary believers in God – that God made the world and keeps it going'.[3] It has also been said that although what the Bible says about God and the world is not metaphysics, 'the Bible does in fact rest upon a profound metaphysical assumption, namely that of the absolute transcendence and independence of God'.[4] Perhaps the cosmological argument, like the ontological argument, can be regarded as an attempt to make explicit the implicit grammar of religious beliefs.

It is at this point, however, that many philosophers of religion find themselves in a dilemma. On the one hand, they are aware of the religious importance of believing in God as the source of the world, as that which gives the world its reality. They see arguments which attempt to prove the existence of God from the existence of the world as efforts to express this truth, and in that way they win their respect. On the other hand, they are convinced philosophically that the ways in which these arguments are often presented are open to unanswerable objections. Philosophers who find themselves in this position may wonder what they ought to say. They may feel that, since the difficulties concerning the arguments are insuperable, there must be something wrong with the religious beliefs which the arguments reflect. On the other hand, since in most cases these beliefs were not arrived at initially by means of philosophy, philosophers may persist in thinking them important. Thus they find themselves torn between religious convictions and philosophical difficulties.

This chapter has the dilemma I have outlined as its central theme. It will be argued that there are insuperable difficulties connected with cosmological arguments, but that these need not touch a belief in God as the source of the world. An attempt will be made to indicate one direction in which to look if we want to understand what might be meant by saying that God is other than the world. Finally, some objections to looking in this direction will be considered.

II

It has been suggested that God is needed as the ultimate explanation of the way things are if intellectual enquiry is to be satisfied. The reason why any particular thing exists must, in the end, be God. Answers in terms of so-called secondary causes are inadequate, since no matter what cause is offered, the question of *its* cause can always be raised. Asking for the cause of any given cause involves one in a pointless infinite regress. Intellectual satisfaction demands as an end to the regress, a cause which cannot itself be caused. God, it is suggested, is such a cause.

It might be thought that this argument is an attempt to express the religious belief that all things depend on God. But what of its difficulties? Is it true that answering ordinary causal questions without reference to God is inadequate? When a child asks his parents where he came from, in what way is an account of procreation an inadequate answer? The fact that the question of origin can be applied in turn to his parents, and then to theirs, does not affect the adequacy of the original answer. The intelligibility and adequacy of the first answer does not depend on grasping a whole series of answers concerning a chain of ancestors.[5] Furthermore, if 'God' *were* given as the answer to all causal questions, the answer could not explain anything. If I ask what caused the window to break, and am given as a reply, 'The same thing that makes your foot itch, the flowers grow, and mountains crumble,' am I any nearer understanding what made the window break?

Those who stress the importance of the infinite causal regress in cosmological arguments, emphasize the intellectual imperative to embark on the regress. But in some cases, allowing the regress to go beyond a certain point reveals, not a commendable persistence in the questioner, but a silliness which fails to recognize when enough is enough. The persistent 'Why?' of the child illustrates this well. The truth is that we constantly accept as adequate answers to the question, 'Why did this happen?' or 'How did this come to be?' A man may ask his wife why there is a mess in front of their house, and be perfectly satisfied when told that the builder's men have been delivering materials for his proposed greenhouse. His acceptance of the answer is bound up with his understanding that delivery of building materials often causes a mess even when reasonable care is exercised. On the other hand, he may think that the mess is excessive, in which case his wife's answer will not satisfy him. Given that a delivery of building materials has been made, he still wants to know why *such* a mess was caused. What determines his asking the further question, however, is not the fact that his wife's original answer *must* lead to it, since, as we have seen, this need not be necessary. What makes him dissatisfied with her answer is that *in the circumstances* it is not a satisfactory explanation. It is the circumstances, that is, the fact of the mess, what is thought to be the degree of untidiness reasonable to expect in the delivery of building materials, and so on, that determine what answer terminates the request for explanations.

Someone who agreed that God need not be referred to in answering ordinary causal questions might still insist on the importance of transcendental explanations. The reason why we have failed to see their importance, he might say, is because we have failed to recognize the proper object of the explanations. If we assume that the existence of particular things needs a transcendental explanation we are mistaken. What such an explanation brings us to understand is the existence of the world itself. The question to which 'God' is the immediate answer is not 'How did this particular state of affairs come to be?' but 'How did the world come to be?' The emphasis on *the world's* dependence on God seeks to do justice to the religious belief that God created the world, but it inherits new difficulties.

It may seem that in asking how the world came to be, we are asking for details of some kind of process or development. But how can this be so? One important difficulty arises from the fact that we are not asking a question about anything in particular. If we ask how a particular thing came to be we can make two assumptions. First, we can assume the existence of something other than the thing in question which brought it to be. But if we ask how everything came to be, how can we appeal to something other than 'everything' to explain its existence? Second, we can assume that any particular thing might not have been. If all the members of a class of things might cease to exist, one can say that this class of things might cease to exist also. But it must be remembered that we are talking about a particular class of things. It is tempting to think of 'all there is' as a class of things, and to argue that since everything that exists might cease to exist, 'all there is' might cease to exist also. Just as we can ask, 'Why should *this* exist?' assuming that there might have been nothing, so we can ask, 'Why should the world exist?' and assume that there might have been nothing. What I find difficult to understand is what 'nothing' means used in this absolute sense.

If we say that 'everything' may cease to exist, we seem to be assuming that the world can be regarded as a thing or as a class of things. One of the difficulties of thinking of the world as a class of things has to do with the criteria by which we determine whether things belong to a particular class or not. The criteria for what is to count as a thing vary with the contexts in which things are individuated. The criteria of individuation will depend on the activities men are engaged in, what their interests are, how they view situations, what they want to find out, and so on. The members of a class satisfy the criteria of membership for that class. But there are no common criteria to determine what is to count as belonging to the world. 'Everything' is not a class of things. This conclusion is underlined by noting that the notion of class entails the notion of a limit, and a distinction between things inside and outside the limit. But when we speak of things being in the world, we do not mean to contrast them with other things which are outside the world. If we ask whether there are certain things in the world, is not this another way of asking whether these things are real? But if inclusion in the world were akin to inclusion in a class, we should have to assume that certain things do or could exist outside the world, which would amount to saying that unreal things do or could exist.

There are difficulties too in thinking of the world as a thing. It has been suggested 'that what is in fact essential to the "Five Ways" is something tantamount to treating the world as a great big object'.[6] But can the world be so treated? Has the world the unity of an object? If it has, it ought to be possible to identify the world demonstratively. In order to do so, however, we should have to determine that the world is the thing it is and not another thing. Any object or group of objects is individuated against a background of other objects. But against what background do we individuate the world? If 'everything' is thought to be a thing, we cannot answer the question, '*This* thing as distinct from what?'

Some philosophers have tried to overcome all these difficulties by stressing the uniqueness of the world's dependence on God. We simply see that the world is contingent – by means of an intuition perhaps. No such appeal to uniqueness or intuition will solve the difficulties. This is because *what* we are said to see or intuit is not at all unique, but depends for its intelligibility on conditions which are not satisfied when we talk about the world. It is not by 'seeing' something to be contingent, or by having an intuition to that effect, that we understand what is meant by the contingency of a thing. We may see or intuit that the existence of something is contingent and be mistaken. What makes the existence of an object contingent is the fact that it depends on something other than itself for its existence. To say in this context that the world is contingent, entails the possibility of the world's ceasing to exist or not having existed. Thus we are brought back to our previous problems. Similar difficulties arise if we say that the world bears the self-authenticating mark of its Maker. An artefact may bear the mark of its maker, but the mark is not self-authenticating. We are acquainted with conventions for marking products, and when we see the mark we know what it means. This is not to say that we have to check that an 'artefact' was made every time we see one, but the appropriateness of calling it an artefact depends on the possibility of such a check being made. So, however we may claim to intuit the dependence of the world on its Maker, without the possibility of an independent check on how the world was made, such claims remain unintelligible.

Some philosophers, recognizing the difficulties we have mentioned, advocate philosophical agnosticism in face of the request for an explanation of the world's existence. Although they think that the theistic answer to this request is untenable, and although all known forms of explanation do not apply to it, they are not prepared to say that the request is meaningless. This is because

If there were a reason-for-the-existence-of-the-world, it would be so distinctive, that it could not be assimilated to any other types of reason known to us. It would be a cosmological reason exclusively. It would not have to do, in any way, with actions, constructions, beliefs, statements, events, or regularities. It would have to do exclusively with the existence of the world and with nothing else. It would not be a typical reason, or a reason that would apply to a class of objects, as is the case with other senses of 'reason'. There would be no recurrent or multiple instances of some type of entity to which it could apply.[7]

The difficulty, however, is to know what meaning *could* be given to 'a reason-for-the-existence-of-the world'. It will not do to appeal to the fact that all *kinds* of explanations are distinctive, and suggest that the explanation of the world's existence will be distinctive too. Although what is to count as an explanation will depend on the context in which an explanation is sought, any explanation, if it is to serve its purpose, will have to be other than what it explains. But how can there be anything other than the world? Until this question is answered, it is difficult to see what meaning can be given to the request for an explanation of the world's existence. It will not do to suggest, as Munitz does, that the request can be given a minimal meaning since *if* there were a reason for the world's existence, it would serve to explain, uniquely, the existence of the world.[8] The difficulty is logically prior to this hypothetical assumption. Can Munitz put into an intelligible form what he is agnostic about, or what it makes sense to hope for as a resolution of this agnosticism? I do not think he has overcome the difficulties Hume raised in his *Dialogues Concerning Natural Religion* concerning speculation about the origin of everything. We have no experience of universes being made. We can speculate on whether a structure is a finished or unfinished house because we are acquainted with house-building. But any hypothesis one cares to put forward about the origin of everything is as good as any other; nothing counts for or against such hypotheses. Hume's observations can be viewed as logical points, since to say that a given hypothesis is as good as any other one cares to mention, and that nothing counts either for or against it, is to deny that it is a genuine hypothesis at all.

So far we have been concerned with well-known difficulties which are internal to arguments which seek to move from the world to God. Even waiving these, however, there are certain external difficulties which anyone who assents to these arguments must face. The external difficulties occur because the conclusions arrived at seem inadequate when compared with certain features of Christian belief. Arguments to establish that God is the cause of the world often look like hypotheses about the origin of things. But a great many believers would not be content to regard the existence of God as an hypothesis, as something which may or may not be true. For them, their fundamental beliefs are absolutes, not hypotheses. In any case, to what extent is the question of the *origin* of things essential to Christian belief? Does any past time depend on God in any sense other than the present does? Is it by coming to value a theory about the origin of things that one comes to see what is meant by acknowledging God as one's Creator? We might recognize a first cause and ask, 'So what?'. Can one recognize God as one's Creator and ask the same question? There may come a time when people no longer believe in God, but that is not akin to a time when a theory is no longer believed. At some future time, people may believe that smoking is not a contributory cause of cancer, having once thought that it was. What they no longer believe will still be intelligible to them; intelligible, but false. Even though a particular theory is no longer believed, others of the

45

same kind are. People will still know what it means to theorize about causal connections. But if a time comes when people no longer believe in God, what other beliefs *of the same kind* will people continue to hold? If a people lost their belief in God, belief in God is not 'intelligible but false' for them, but unintelligible. To no longer believe in God is not to disbelieve one thing among many of the same kind, but to see no sense in *anything* of that kind. What has become meaningless is not some feature of a form of life, but a form of life as such. If we were seeking an analogy between science and religion in this context, despite important differences, we ought to compare the time when God is no longer believed in, not with a time when a scientific theory is no longer held, but with a time when people can make nothing of the practice of science.

The internal and external difficulties surrounding the arguments we have considered constitute the dilemma of the philosopher who recognizes them, but does not want to conclude that belief in God as the source of the world's reality is meaningless. Most of the difficulties were connected with the desire to ask of the world the same causal questions that one can ask of particular things. Defending the possibility of asking such questions, Geach says, 'Why should we not raise them? It would be childish to say that the world is too big for such questions to be reasonable; and to say the world is all-inclusive would be to beg the question – God would not be included in the world.'[9] The crucial question, however, concerns *the sense* in which God is not included in the world. Is there a sense in which God is other than the world which is not touched by any of the difficulties we have considered? I believe there is.

III

When someone asks why there is anything at all, he need not be asking for the details of any process or development. His question may be about the sense, meaning, or reality of everything. The question may be posed in a general way, or it may be asked about something quite specific. The question Dmitri asks in his dream in *The Brothers Karamazov* is quite specific: he wants to know why a baby is crying. Yet, having been given all the explanations of the child's condition, of the disasters which had befallen it and its family, Dmitri still feels the urge to ask *Why?* 'And he felt that, though his questions were unreasonable and senseless, yet he wanted to ask just that; and he had to ask it just in that way.' Although the question has a specific reference, it is still a question about the sense of things. The traditional distinction between the cosmological argument and the argument from design obscures this fact. The former, it is said, takes as its starting-point the fact that there is anything at all, whereas the latter begins from the fact that what there is has some features rather than others, as if the perplexities which the respective arguments try to meet must be different. But, as we have seen, concern about the particular may nevertheless be a question about the meaning of the world.[10] In this context, questions about the meaning of the world and questions about the meaning of life are one and the same.

But are we rid of the objections of the last section of the chapter if, instead of asking, 'What is the cause of everything?' we ask, 'What is the meaning of everything?'? We know how to cope with questions which ask

47

for the meaning of *this* or *that*. We may not be able to answer such questions because of our ignorance, but the questions do not baffle us, although the answers may. We know the *kind* of questions they are. But what are we asking for when we ask for the meaning of everything? If we want to give an adequate explanation of the meaning of *this*, we must refer to something *other than this*. But if we ask for the meaning of everything, what can we refer to which is other than everything?[11] So it seems that in questions about causality and in questions about meaningfulness, when the world is the subject of the questions, the same difficulty faces us: the difficulty of asking of the world the same questions that can be asked about particular things.

Does it follow that it is meaningless to ask for the meaning of the world? No; all that follows is that the meaning cannot be located outside the world. This difficulty is not insuperable, since, often, what is held to make life meaningful and worthwhile is not something other than or beyond life, but an emphasis of certain features of life itself. We may say of someone, 'His work is his life' or 'He lives for his family'. It may be the case that a single incident of great sorrow or great joy determines a person's view of the world.[12] A routine of monotonous regularity may convince a person of the worthlessness and triviality of life. In all these cases, how someone sees the world is determined by the emphasis he gives to certain features of his world, which he believes to be important or trivial.

But how does any of this help us to understand what many Christians want to say about the world? These believers *do* want to say that the meaning of the world lies outside the world – namely, in God. There seems to be a clash between such statements and a general thesis which can be extracted from Hume's *Dialogues Concerning Natural Religion* – namely, that there is no need to go beyond the natural order to explain it. Hume's objections hold against any attempt to extend to a reality or Being said to be other than the world ways of talking which are only intelligible within the world.

But why should anyone think that it is religiously important to show that Hume is mistaken? What if Hume's objections could be overcome, and we were able to think of another world which is a logical extension of this one, of a God who is the cause of everything in some way akin to the ways in which other causes cause particular things, and of a divine agency which operates beyond the world in a way akin to human agencies? Why should any of this be thought to be important for religion? If this world is meaningless, why should another world, which is a logical extension of it, be any less meaningless? For example, we may be tempted, through confusing eternity with duration, to think of eternal life as a life which is after this one, and a logical extension of it. But, as Wittgenstein pointed out:

> Not only is there no guarantee of the temporal immortality of the human soul, that is to say of its eternal survival after death; but, in any case, this assumption completely fails to accomplish the purpose for which it has always been intended. Or is some riddle solved by my surviving for ever? Is not this eternal life as much of a riddle as our present life?[13]

If we look at what has been said in Christian traditions by great religious teachers and thinkers about the relation between this world and another world which is said to be the true reality, we are not struck by the continuity between them. On the contrary, what strikes us is the radical discontinuity of the relation. It is said that before a man can see this world in the light of a reality which is beyond it, he must undergo a radical change. The analogies of birth and death are used to stress the nature of this change.[14] Before a man can enter the world, the kingdom of God, he must die to this world. Or, to express the point in terms of the other analogy: before a man can begin to comprehend the reality which is beyond the world, he must be born again. Man becomes a member of this world by being born of woman; he becomes a member of the other world by being born from above, born of God. I am suggesting that what these analogies are trying to convey is not open to the objections we considered in the second section of this chapter.

But what sense does this way of talking have? It is not a way of talking which is unfamiliar in philosophy. Plato, in the *Phaedo*, speaks of the strivings of the soul to turn away from the temporal to the eternal. At first this may seem to be an exhortation to turn from slavery to desire and pay heed to moral considerations. Certainly, this is involved in what Plato is saying. But there is more to it than that. He calls the turning away from the temporal to the eternal a form of purification or the practice of dying, and wants to contrast things seen from the world's point of view with things seen from the standpoint of the eternal. This way of talking goes beyond ethics in its usual sense. In short, Plato is expounding a religious morality. The man who pays attention to moral considerations will not worry if he does not attain the worldly advance which immoral action would have brought him. Still, he does have certain moral expectations. He has certain rights which may or may not be satisfied. Sometimes he will see that his rights ought not to be satisfied, and that competing rights have stronger claims. At other times his rights are wrongfully neglected. At times such as these, he will feel harmed, and expect some kind of restitution. Thus, in their different ways, the man whose aim is to satisfy his desires and the man who upholds certain moral principles are both concerned about how the world is treating them. Both, in Wittgenstein's phrase, see 'objects as it were from the midst of them'[15] and in so doing see things from the world's point of view. Much of what is meant by seeing things from the point of view of the eternal can be grasped by understanding what it means to die to the expectations created by desire or moral rights.

Many religious teachers speak of the necessity of 'dying to oneself'. Often they are referring to the refusal to use one's power when one is the stronger member of an unequal relationship. When the inequality is marked as in slavery, the weaker member is in danger of ceasing to be a person. In order to renounce one's power one must not fix one's attention on *how* people are: useful or useless for one, desirable or undesirable, morally deserving or undeserving, but on the fact *that* they are. This is a prerequisite of compassion. When it is achieved in the presence of suffering, the giver is able to give without feeling that he has done anything deserving of praise, and the sufferer is able to receive without feeling bought or degraded. It might be said that in this attitude people are seen, not as the world sees them, but as God sees them.[16]

51

The believer, if his faith is at all deep, is not concerned with his rights. He is not concerned with receiving thanks for the good he does, or recompense for the harm he suffers. What he considers to be advantage, disadvantage, happiness or misery, is determined by his relationship to the love of God. Those who see things from the midst of them, from the world's point of view, will find his attitude difficult to understand. Polus found Socrates hard to understand. He argued that advantage and disadvantage are contingently related to goodness and badness. Neither he nor Callicles could understand how Socrates could say, 'I should be a fool, Callicles, if I didn't realize that in this state anything may happen to anybody' and go on to say without contradiction, 'All is well.' Socrates is saying that the well-being of the lover of the good does not depend on how things are for him in the world, on what is the case, since he says that all is well *whatever is the case.* There is a striking parallel between these remarks, and Kierkegaard's attempt to show the sense in which eternal love cannot be deceived. Kierkegaard argues that temporal love, whether it be self-love, friendship, love of parents, or love of a husband or wife, depends on how things are in the world, and can suffer defeat. Eternal love, love of human beings as such, although it believes all things, cannot suffer defeat since, Kierkegaard argues, only the man who ceases to love is deceived. The world's way of regarding the matter will be radically different. In the eyes of the world, only a fool believes all things. Kierkegaard does not deny any of the obvious deceptions which the world may cite as evidence. Yet he continues to say that the man who continues to believe all things in love cannot be deceived, just as Socrates continued to say that all was well despite his recognition of what Athens might have in store for a lover of the good. Plato and Kierkegaard would have approved of Wittgenstein's remark that ethics has nothing to do with punishment and reward in the usual sense of these terms, or that if there is a connection between them, it is because there is an ethical reward and an ethical punishment which reside in the action itself.[17] The internal relation of which Wittgenstein speaks is illustrated in the following analysis by Kierkegaard:

> . . . he who in love forgets himself, forgets his sufferings in order to think of another's, forgets all his wretchedness in order to think of another's . . . truly, such a person is not forgotten. There is one who thinks of him, God in heaven; or love thinks of him. God is love, and when a human being because of love forgets himself, how then should God forget him! No, while the lover forgets himself and thinks of the other person, God thinks of the lover . . . the lover who forgets himself, is remembered by love. There is one who thinks of him, and in this way it comes about that the lover gets what he gives.[18]

So far I have been trying to illustrate what some religious teachers have meant by a love for other people which is *other than the world*. There is a parallel between this and what the same religious teachers want to say about the fortunes or misfortunes which may befall one. Here, too, there is an all-important distinction between *how* things are, and *that* things are. The Book of Job illustrates this distinction well. At first, Job wants an explanation of the misfortunes which have befallen him. What he comes to recognize, however, is the necessity for renouncing the desire for explanations and consolations. By coming to see that the contingencies which had befallen him had no explanation, Job is delivered from dependence upon them. The indiscriminate nature of fortune and misfortune is used by him to teach himself that he is nothing: he ceases to be the centre of his world. Simone Weil expresses the point well: 'If I thought that God sent me suffering by an act of His will and for my good, I should think that I was something, and I should miss the chief use of suffering which is to teach me that I am nothing. It is therefore essential to avoid all such thoughts, but it is necessary to love God through the suffering.'[19] What Job came to was the possibility of loving the world as such, to what the mystics have called love of the beauty of the world. The beauty of the world in this context does not admit of a contrast with the ugliness of the world, since it comprises both its beauty and its ugliness understood relatively. The absolute beauty of the world can be equated with the sense of the world. It is not by emphasizing some features of the world rather than others, as all arguments from design are forced to do, that the believer arrives at love of the world. Love of the world as such is arrived at by taking account of all the features of the world. The Hebrew stresses that God is not only the God who sees the sparrow fall, but also the God who creates the darkness 'wherein all the beasts of the forest do creep forth. The young lions roar after their prey, and seek their meat from God.'[20] *Any* event can lead the believer to God.

Both with love of nature and love of human beings, the attitude of the deeply religious man is not determined by looking at things from the midst of them. To

54

say that his attitude is other than this is what is meant
by saying that his attitude is other than the world's way
of regarding things. His view is of the world as a whole,
and determines the nature of the world for him. His
world is a different world from that of the man who sees
objects from the midst of them. *How* the world is is the
same for both of them, but what they make of the world
is different. This phrase, 'what they make of the world',
has led some philosphers to speak of religious beliefs as
attitudes to life. In some contexts this way of talking is
unobjectionable, but it can be misleading. It may suggest that religious responses to the world are in the same
logical category as 'bearing things with equanimity',
'making the best of a bad situation', 'taking a long-
term view of things', etc. What such a categorization
neglects is the way in which the worship of God makes
the believer's relationship to other people and the events
which befall him substantially different; that is to say,
without his belief he could not be said to have the same
relationship or experience the same events. The
believer's worship 'must make the world a wholly
different one. The world must, so to speak, wax or wane
as a whole. As if by accession or loss of meaning.'[21]

Someone might point out, however, that religious
views of the world are not the only views of the world as
a whole. There are many such views. If this is accepted,
why should the religious view of the world be called
other than the world? The facts may be the same for two
people: their child has been killed. But for one it makes
life meaningless, whereas the other says he must try to
make the best of it. Or consider how something more
trivial, such as being passed over for promotion, can,
for one man, colour the whole of his life, and for another

55

make no difference whatever. It cannot be denied that the persons whose lives are coloured by these events have attitudes to life as a whole. Yet, although their attitudes have not been determined by a weighing up of pros and cons, they have been determined, nevertheless, by some feature of the world. Although one feature is given great emphasis, it is still a case of assessing things from the midst of them.

The reason why love of God is said to be *other than* the world is, as I have tried to illustrate, because it entails dying to the world's way of regarding things. On one level, this can be regarded as dying to the world. On another, it can be called love of the world. This is because 'world' in the first sense refers to what we have called seeing objects from the midst of them. The love of God, which involves dying to this world, does not mean that the believer has no regard for the world. On the contrary, the love of God is manifested in the believer's relationship to people and things. In this sense, he can be said to have a love of the world. To see the world as God's world, would, primarily,[22] be to possess this love. To say that God created the world would not be to put forward a theory, hypothesis, or explanation, of the world. It might be said that 'Saying of the world that it is created stands to the fact of its being extended in a way analogous to saying of a body that it is a person stands to its having three dimensions'.[23]

Despite the objections we considered earlier, it might be said that the attempt of cosmological arguments to move from the fact that *anything* exists to the reality of God has within it the seeds of the religious beliefs we have been grappling with – namely, the insistence that it is by contemplating the existence of human beings and natural events *as such* that one comes to see what is meant by God's being other than the world.

IV

I am aware that there are internal difficulties involved in the position I have tried to maintain. I shall not attempt to meet these difficulties in this chapter, but they ought to be mentioned. The three I have in mind all arise from the emphasis I have given to the radical discontinuity between this world and 'the other world', between the temporal and the eternal.

I wanted to say that the man who loves God cannot be touched by the world, by how things are. Socrates wanted to say that all is well whatever is the case. Kierkegaard wanted to say that whatever is the case, eternal love cannot suffer defeat. Wittgenstein wanted to say that he had an experience of feeling absolutely safe, and that nothing could harm him. The biggest objection to this way of talking comes from the fact that affliction can destroy the possibility of loving God.[24] So it seems that the believer cannot say that all is well no matter what happens, since if certain things happen he can no longer believe. On the other hand, would believers say that God had deserted a man if the affliction which destroys his faith is itself the consequence of loving God?

The other objections centre around the notions of religious difficulties and religious strivings. If the break between the temporal and the eternal were as radical as I have suggested, how could there be any difficulties or strivings to meet them? Belief would be an 'all-or-nothing' affair. Clearly, this is not the case.[25]

Despite these difficulties, I should still want to argue

that I have indicated one *direction* in which to look to see what some believers mean when they say that God is other than the world. The indication of this direction is only the beginning, but where we should begin is precisely what is in dispute in contemporary philosophy of religion. Before ending, I want to mention briefly two related objections against looking in the direction I have indicated.

It might be said that because I have sought the meaning of God's otherness in contexts where this notion has its life, I have in some way identified God and the world. R. W. Hepburn suggests that in appealing to the meaning a religious belief may have in people's lives, 'we are speaking only of observable phenomena, and of how we interpret, what we "make of", those phenomena'.[26] Hepburn is suggesting that no matter how much attention we pay to religious forms of life, this must be inadequate, since we are still referring to a feature of the world, rather than to a God who transcends and is independent of the world. Hepburn says:

> I want, in fact, to suggest that the Cosmological Argument – or some transformation of it – is not just one approach to apologetics among others, one to be distinguished altogether from apologetics based on historical revelation. It is an indispensable part of any Christian apologetics whatever, including those that centre on revelation. For . . . at some point appeal must be made away from the finite and historical locus of revelation to the infinite and eternal God to whom these allegedly testify.[27]

Hepburn's objection confuses epistemological and religious questions.[28] To say that one must refer to the

58

life of religious institutions to see the meaning of religious beliefs is not to say that those beliefs say anything about institutions. To say that *the meaning* of God's reality is to be found *in* the world, is not to deny that God is *other than* the world in the sense important to religion. It *is* religiously important to distinguish between God and the world, but to see what this distinction comes to one must give some examples of the ways in which it is used.

The second objection which is sometimes made against the way I have argued is that it denies the objective reality of God. The term 'objective reality' is a hazy one. The objector may be suggesting that the believer creates his belief, or decides that it should be the kind of thing it is. This is obviously not the case. The believer is taught religious beliefs. He does not create a tradition, but is born into one. He cannot say whatever he likes about God, since there are criteria which determine what it makes sense to say. These criteria may develop or change partly as the result of personal decisions. But not anything can count as a religious decision or a religious development.

The objector may claim that if one argues as I have done, it is impossible to be mistaken about the nature of God. This is not true. One may think one is worshipping God when in fact one is worshipping idols. Imagine how, in the context of the kind of belief I have tried to outline, pride and humility could be interwoven in a man. This alone is sufficient to show how intricate a form mistakes can take in religion. To see what a mistake in religious faith amounts to, we should have to consider what is meant by the presence, lack, and development, of religious understanding.

59

From World to God?

The objector who accuses me of denying the objective reality of God may have in mind a statement which I should support – namely, the statement that God is not an object. That is a statement of grammar. Those who deny it, I suggest, speak of God in a way which is a logical extension of ways in which we speak about human beings. If God is a thing He is finite; and a finite God satisfies the needs neither of religion nor theology. But a finite God satisfies many philosophers of religion. The God over whom our debates rage is the finite God of Cleanthes, whose inadequacies Hume exposed long ago.

References

1. See *Philosophical Review*, lxix (1960); reprinted in Malcolm, N., *Knowledge and Certainty*, Prentice Hall: Englewood Cliffs, N.J., 1963; in *The Existence of God*, ed. by Hick, John, Macmillan, 1964; and in *Religion and Understanding*, ed. Phillips, D. Z., Basil Blackwell, 1967.
2. *Our Knowledge of God*, O.U.P., 1939, 141.
3. Geach, Peter, 'Aquinas' in *Three Philosophers*, by Anscombe, G. E. M., and Geach, Peter, Basil Blackwell, 1961, 109.
4. Mascall, E. L., *Existence and Analogy*, Longmans, 1949, 18.
5. See Geach, *op. cit.*, 111.
6. Geach, *ibid.*, 112.
7. Munitz, Milton K., *The Mystery of Existence*, Appleton-Century-Crofts, 1965, 212–13.
8. *Ibid.*, 249.
9. Geach, *op. cit.*, 113.
10. For further examples and discussion of this point see my book, *The Concept of Prayer*, Routledge & Kegan Paul, 1965, ch. 5 and 6.
11. See Wisdom, John, 'The Meanings of the Questions of Life', in *Paradox and Discovery*, Basil Blackwell, 1965.
12. *Cf.* Wisdom, John, 'Religious Belief', *op. cit.*, 50.
13. Wittgenstein, Ludwig, *Tractatus Logico-Philosophicus*, trans.

Pears, D. F., and McGuinness, B. F., Routledge & Kegan Paul, 1961, 6.4312.

14. For an illuminating discussion of these analogies see Poteat, W. H., 'Birth, Suicide and the Doctrine of Creation: An Exploration of Analogies', *Mind*, lxviii (1959), and 'I Will Die', *Philosophical Quarterly*, 9 (1959), both reprinted in *Religion and Understanding*.

15. *Notebooks 1914–1916*, ed. by Wright, G. H. von, and Anscombe, G. E. M., trans. by Anscombe, G. E. M., 1961, 83.

16. *Cf.* Jones, J. R., 'Love as Perception of Meaning', in *Religion and Understanding*.

17. See *Notebooks*, 78; *Tractatus*, 6.422.

18. *Works of Love*, trans. Hong, Howard and Edna, Collins, 1962, 262.

19. *Gravity and Grace*, trans. Craufurd, Emma, Routledge & Kegan Paul, 1952, 101.

20. Ps. civ. 20. *Cf.* the use made of this quotation in Norman Kemp Smith's 'Is Divine Existence Credible?', *Proc. British Academy*, 1931; reprinted in *Religion and Understanding*.

21. Wittgenstein, *Notebooks*, 73. *Cf. Tractatus*, 6.43. *Cf.* also the use of these made by McGuinness, B. F., 'The Mysticism of the *Tractatus*' in *Philosophical Review*, July 1966, 318. This paper appeared too late to be given serious attention, but I am puzzled as to why McGuinness thinks that Wittgenstein's remarks are not consistent with theistic mysticism.

22. I say 'primarily' because of the possibility of other responses to seeing the world as God's, e.g. rebellion, fear, or aspiration.

23. Poteat, W. H., 'Birth, Suicide, and the Doctrine of Creation: an Exploration of Analogies', *Religion and Understanding*, 138.

24. *Cf.* Winch, Peter, 'Can a Good Man be Harmed?' *Proc. Arist. Soc.*, 1965–6, 69–70.

25. I discuss this difficulty at length in 'Religious Beliefs and Language Games'. See pp. 77–110 of this volume.

26. 'From World to God', *Mind*, lxxii (1963), 40.

27. *Ibid.*, 43.

28. See 'Religion and Epistemology: Some Contemporary Confusions', pp. 123–45 of this volume, for a discussion of what I take to be examples of this confusion in the writings of Professors Hick and Hepburn, and Bishop Ramsey.

IV Religious Belief and Philosophical Enquiry

It might be worth saying at the outset that the first chapter of my book, *The Concept of Prayer*, was written last. Some philosophers have spoken as if I had in my possession first something called a general philosophical position, and then applied this to the life of prayer. Professor Hick and Dr Palmer are tempted sometimes to speak in this way.[1] This is quite incorrect. What I started with was a cluster of problems concerning prayer which puzzled me very much: How does the believer know that there is anyone listening to him when he prays? When believers talk of God, in what sense does He understand what they say? Is talking to God like talking to another human being? Believers confess their sins to God, they give thanks to Him, and ask Him for various things, but what do confessing, thanking, and asking come to in this context? These, and other questions, were the ones which excited me. I tried to answer them by taking as examples prayers which Christians have heard often enough, and asking what it means to pray those prayers. It was only after attempting to do this that I asked myself why some philosophers have concluded that these activities are radically confused or meaningless.

Part of the answer seems to be that these philosophers

are not immune to a craving for generality, a desire to give an all-embracing unitary account of reality. In their appeals to ordinary language they assume that there is a paradigmatic use of 'ordinary' which can be used to judge all uses of language. According to them, different kinds of discourse can be judged by their success or failure in corresponding to reality. This assumes, of course, that 'corresponding to reality' can mean something independent of any mode of discourse. What I tried to urge was that the distinction between the real and the unreal does not come to the same thing in every context. To think otherwise is to fall into a deep confusion about the relation between language and reality. To illustrate this, I quoted a crucial passage from Peter Winch's article, 'Understanding a Primitive Society':

> Reality is not what gives language sense. What is real and what is unreal shows itself *in* the sense that language has. Further, both the distinction between the real and the unreal and the concept of agreement with reality themselves belong to our language.[2]

Commenting on this passage, I said:

> One can say *within* any such context, whether it be science or religion, 'This is the rule which *must* be observed, this is the meaning which a word *must* have if it is to belong to this conceptual family.' But when philosophers say, 'This is the meaning which a word *must have*' without specifying any context, they are guilty of arbitrary linguistic legislation. The 'must' is not a logical 'must', but simply the 'must' of their own preferences, or the 'must' of one context which

63

they have elevated, consciously or unconsciously, to be a standard for all others.[3]

There is little doubt that Palmer, in his article, has misunderstood the import of these remarks. He says that if one assumes that whereas one can make mistakes within religion or science, it makes no sense to ask whether religion as such or science as such are mistakes, 'one will have to think of some other name for the sort of mistake that religion, or science, or magic, or croquet might turn out to be'. But if Palmer had *really* seen the truth of the above argument, he would not be faced with the task of finding a name for the kind of mistake religion might turn out to be, since he would have recognized the unintelligibility of speaking of something turning out to be a mistake in this context.

But, of course, Palmer does not really believe what he says he has assumed. He asks, 'but *who says* that religion is a distinct and separable field, etc., etc.?'. I find this question extremely odd. It is not a matter of anyone *saying* that there are differences between modes of discourse, but *looking* to see whether there are any such differences, and if there are, *showing* their character. It is not at all clear to me whether Palmer wants to deny that there are different modes of discourse. He asks who is to decide what frontiers exist between modes of discourse, and whether the activity of deciding will itself be a mode of discourse. Palmer says: 'To avoid this regress, I suggest that we take Winch's argument with a pinch of salt.' The pinch of salt recommended turns out to be the recognition that 'given several rules of logic, their domains need not be *either* co-extensive *or* mutually exclusive. They may interpenetrate and overlap.' But the pinch of salt is unnecessary, since Palmer must have forgotten a fact which I noted in *The Concept of Prayer*[4] – namely, that Winch recognizes that the precise expression of his point would have to be more complicated to allow for 'the overlapping character of different modes of social life'.[5] Of course, there will be no strict lines of demarcation between different modes of discourse at many points, but Palmer is misled into thinking that it follows from this that we need an umpire to decide whether there are any differences at all. He is like the man who, because he could not determine the fixed boundary between night and day, denied that there were differences between them.

Palmer complains that it is premature to claim that religious beliefs make up a distinctive mode of discourse because no 'satisfactory and consistent logic' has 'yet been worked out for discourse in this area'. I am not at all clear what Palmer means by a 'satisfactory and consistent logic'. What would be the rules of consistency? Palmer gives no examples. He says that 'For each rule of logic, we must try to discover the appropriate domain.' Palmer seems to view logical rules as a direct gift from God for which we must try to find a home: some will have homes everywhere, some will have homes only in certain places – but will some be homeless? – I just don't know, since Palmer gives no examples of what he has in mind. Previously, Palmer had quoted Winch's remark that 'Criteria of logic are not a direct gift of God, but arise out of, and are only intelligible in the context of, ways of living or modes of social life'.[6] So the above comments by Palmer simply beg the question at issue. It is difficult to see how he can avoid doing so without using examples to establish his points. Furthermore, when Palmer, referring to religion, says that no 'satisfactory and consistent logic' has 'yet been worked out for discourse in this area', what *area* has he in mind? If he says *this* area as opposed to *that* one, then he seems to have the ability to identify religious practices unaided by his hitherto unattained 'satisfactory and consistent logic'.

Why is Palmer reluctant to say that religious beliefs make up a distinctive mode of discourse? For him, to say this would be to accept a version of what he calls 'the inseparability thesis' – namely, 'that only believers can understand the statements made and the concepts involved in professions of religious belief'. Palmer says that 'in order to decide whether to believe what these people say, I shall try to understand it first!' I am afraid he has not succeeded in his task, despite the variety of versions offered. This is because Palmer fails to distinguish between philosophical and religious understanding. When he attributes to me the view that only believers can understand the statements made and the concepts involved in professions of religious belief, he could mean so many things. Does he mean that if you are a religious believer, you have a philosophical understanding of the concepts involved in religious practices? If so, I cannot see how the view can be attributed to me, since I said quite explicitly in *The Concept of Prayer*,

> A believer is asked to give an account of prayer. . . .
> What he is asked to do is to give a conceptual account
> of the kind of activity prayer is. Often, in face of such
> a request, the believer is lost.[7]

So belief in God does not entail philosophical understanding. But perhaps Palmer had something else in mind. Perhaps he thought I was saying that only philo-

sophers who are religious believers can understand anything about religious beliefs. But, then, I had said of the
question, 'What is the grammar of our idea of God:
what can we say and what cannot we say about God?'
that to some extent it was formal and theoretical:

> One can see what kind of account religious beliefs call
> for without understanding a great deal about the
> *religious* significance of these beliefs. . . . One can
> know the moves in chess without having a love for the
> game, and to some extent this is possible in philosophy
> of religion: one can go far in saying what God *cannot*
> be if any sense is to be made of religion at all, but to
> say what *is* meant by belief in God, one must take
> account of what God means to religious believers;
> one must have some feeling for the game. We must
> ask what worshipping an eternal God means in the
> way of life in which it flourishes.[8]

My conclusion might be expressed as follows:

> If it is possible to make philosophically correct moves
> in this context, without feeling a love for the game, I
> think it may also be possible to have a love for the
> game, and yet to make all the wrong philosophical
> moves.[9]

So quite clearly, I distinguish between religious and
philosophical understanding. What I wish to urge is
that one can only give a satisfactory account of religious
beliefs if one pays attention to the roles they play in
people's lives. By comparing these roles with others one
can bring out the grammar of religious belief. This is
what I tried to do by comparing confessing, thanking,
and asking in prayer, with confessing, thanking, and

asking in other contexts. In doing this, I think Palmer
believes that I am indulging in apologetics. This is a
confusion. The philosopher must see what it *means* to
believe in God in order to give an account of agnosticism, atheism, rebellion, fear of God, etc. These are
religious phenomena; they would not exist if there were
no religion. Palmer has made the mistake of thinking
that I equate believers and worshippers. The class of
believers is wider than the class of worshippers; all
worshippers are believers, but not all believers are
worshippers. Palmer's depiction of my efforts as that of
a nervous apologist pulling up the drawbridge whenever the going gets tough and saying to the non-believer,
'You cannot understand,' misses *completely* the philosophical questions at issue. Clarifying the grammar of
religious beliefs is important, not simply in order to see
what worship means, but also in order to see what
rebellion, resentment, fear, dread, etc., may come to in
this context. Let me try to sum the matter up in this
way: to try to see the meaning of religious beliefs is not
to advocate what meaning they should have in people's
lives. Love of God is not the only form of religious belief,
but I believe it is the primary form. That is a *grammatical*
observation. We could not have anything we know as
Christianity if the other forms of belief were to become
the rule. You have to rebel *against something*, you have to
be afraid *of something*. Love of God is logically prior to
the other forms of belief.

The issues which bothered Palmer also worry Professor Hick. To some extent, his worries too come from a
failure to distinguish between religious and philosophical understanding. For example, Hick thinks that
I deny that there is any question as to whether God

exists, as distinct from the question whether people have the concept of God. He quotes me as saying:

> What [the believer] learns is religious language; a language which he participates in along with other believers. What I am suggesting is that to know how to use this language is to know God.

I was referring there to the way in which religion is taught, the way we come to see what is meant by God through stories, pictures, etc. It might be said that when children form conceptions of God they have a primitive theology which determines what can and what cannot be said about God. The theology is implicit in religious language. It makes no sense to ask which came first, the language or the theology. A theology determines what can and what cannot be said in the language without being prior to it.[10] When I said that 'to know how to use this language is to know God' I was referring to the language of worship, contemplation, and religious practices. To *use* this language is to worship, to believe in God. So it is highly misleading for Hick to say that I am not concerned with the existence of God, when the very question I am raising concerns the grammar of the reality of God. Hick says:

> In denying . . . that there is a proper question as to whether God exists, and declaring instead that the proper question is whether one has a use for religious language, Phillips appears to assume that the use of religious language does not itself involve belief in the existence of God.

So far as I know, I never raise the question of whether one has a use for religious language. I do not know what the question means! What I *am* saying is that it is *within* religious discourse that we find what is meant by the reality of God.

Because he misconstrues the philosophical issues at stake, Hick misunderstands the point of my comparison of the philosophical treatment of the reality of physical objects with the philosophical treatment of the reality of God. He says that whereas we are all agreed about the reality of the physical world, we are not all agreed about the reality of God. But when *did* we agree about the reality of physical objects? What would it be like to disagree? I know what it means to agree that it is a tree and not a lamp-post that we see in the fog. But when I am facing the tree in normal conditions do I agree that it is a tree? What if everyone else said that it was not a tree? Would I say that I must be mistaken? No. I should think I was mad! We are familiar with situations where we say, 'This is a tree', 'Here is a torn page', 'Here is an ink-bottle' and so on. Our confidence in saying so is not based on evidence. No; such situations are examples of the kind of thing we *mean* by talking about physical objects. Should our confidence in such situations be undermined, the result would not be greater caution on our part, but radical changes in our use of the words 'physical object'.[11] There is no question of justifying the criteria for our use of 'physical object': that is how we *do* use the concept. The comparison with the reality of God was meant to be at this grammatical level. In each case there would be no question of a general justification of the criteria for distinguishing between the real and the unreal.

Of course, if a man does not believe in God we do not say that he is mad. This fact perhaps encourages Hick to think that there can be a justification of the belief in God. He seems to think that the believer and the unbeliever are disagreeing over whether something is a fact or not – namely, the existence of God. Hick says that the reality of God is what Hume called a matter of fact and existence. Furthermore, he seems to know someone called 'the typical religious man' who, when asked, '"Are you assuming that there actually is a Being whom you are addressing (or referring to) and who is eternal, omnipotent, etc.?"' replies unhesitatingly, 'Yes'. Put like that, how could the reply be any different? The suggested, but unstated, alternative is to say that 'God' is an illusion.

I have no doubt, however, that *the same* believers who say that the existence of God is a fact would, if pressed, admit that the discovery of God is not like the discovery of a matter of fact, and that there is no question of God ceasing to exist, of having existed for a certain length of time, or of having come into existence. Hick seems to recognize this when he says, 'There is, to be sure, no question whether God contingently exists.' I should have thought it followed from this that the reality of God cannot be what Hume called a matter of fact and existence. But Hick goes on to say that 'there is a question whether he eternally and independently (i.e. necessarily) exists, in distinction from eternally not existing'. If Hick is equating eternity with duration I find the above question meaningless. If he is not equating them, his question as to whether the notion of an eternal God is real is a question about the intelligibility of the notion. What I am urging is that the intelligibility of the family of language-games covered by the term 'religion' is not assessed by wider criteria of meaningfulness.

Religious Belief and Philosophical Enquiry

As Wittgenstein stressed, a thing can only be a blunder within a particular system.[12] If Hick and Palmer want to say that religion *could* be a blunder, the onus is on them to specify the language-game within which the blunder could occur. Much of their misunderstanding comes from their tendency to think of religious beliefs as hypotheses, or as beliefs which wait on a further external check. Wittgenstein brings out the misunderstanding involved when he asks us to imagine how inappropriate it would be to say of someone who believes in God, 'You only believe – oh well . . .'[13]

The view that there can be no *general* justification of religion is open to many misunderstandings. Hick and Palmer seem to think it means that the believer can say whatever he likes. That is not so. Religious believers make mistakes like anyone else. What they say, *if* it comes under the appropriate criteria of meaningfulness, must answer to these criteria. Hick is right too in saying that certain conceptions of God are confused, e.g. 'Yuri Gagarin's concept of God as an object that he would have observed, had it existed, during his first space flight'. It can be shown to be confused in two ways: first, by reference to what one can reasonably expect to observe in space, and secondly, by reference to what is meant by the reality of God. So far from showing the possibility of an external justification of religious belief by the example of confused beliefs he cites, Hick unwittingly underlines the fact that *it is only by reference to other religious beliefs that the confusion is recognized.*

Hick is not content with conceptual analysis. He wants philosophy to promote, praise, blame, and advocate. Otherwise, he thinks I can have nothing to say about the traditional theistic arguments, the relation

72

between science and religion, the competing truth-claims of various religions, naturalistic theories of religion, etc. But this is not true at all. All these topics and many more are often the source of conceptual confusion: What is meant by a truth-claim in religion? What does it mean to speak of these claims as *competing*? What kind of a problem is the problem of evil? Wherever there is conceptual confusion, there too is the home of conceptual analysis. I cannot argue the question here, but I should want to say that it is Hick's desire to *advocate* in these contexts which constitutes an impurity in philosophy.

Let me return, all too briefly, I fear, to the notion of God's eternity, and in particular to the notion of eternal life as God's life, the life of which believers desire to partake. God is divinely real. Understand what is meant by the divinity of God, and you understand what is meant by the reality of God at the same time.

Hick says that

> The notions of the existence of God and of the factual truth of statements about him are bound up with the principle that any possible history of the universe which satisfies, e.g. 'God loves mankind', must differ experientially from any possible history of the universe which does not satisfy it.

I had said elsewhere, and Hick quotes me, that

> There are some people the truth of whose religion depends on the way things go in their lives. Things may not go well here and now, but unless the ultimate facts, the eschatological situation, are favourable in some sense or other, faith has been a hoax and a

failure. For Hick, the kind of difference religion makes to life is the difference between a set of empirical facts being or not being the case.[14]

I do not want to repeat the objections I made against I. M. Crombie's and Basil Mitchell's version of this view in *The Concept of Prayer*.[15] Instead I shall simply indicate a contrast between this view, and a radically different religious attitude.[16]

People did not need Kant to tell them that the world does not always reward the virtuous. They have asked, 'Why do the wicked prosper?' Christianity speaks of overcoming the world. But in what sense is it overcome? According to Christianity, it is overcome by a certain kind of love, to possess which is to know God and to have eternal life. The believer recognizes that things may not turn out as he would want them to. He must come to terms with that in such a way that, whatever happens, he can still go on. He brings his sins, his desires, his expectations, to God in prayer, and his wish is that none of these things will come between him and the love of God. The love of God is not something he arrives at by a statistical assessment of the facts, but is itself the measure which brings order to whatever is the case; not the order of a plan, but the order or meaningfulness involved in the exercise of love.[17] But for Hick and Palmer things must go in one way rather than the other. They would have difficulty in seeing how Socrates can say, without contradiction, that *anything* may happen to him in Athens, and that *all will be well*. In the eyes of the world, all cannot be well if anything may happen to one. But according to Christianity, on many occasions, what the believer calls 'success' will seem a failure in the

74

eyes of the world, what he calls 'joy' will seem like grief, what he calls 'victory' will seem like certain defeat. So it was, it is said, at the Cross of Christ.[18]

I have spent my time trying to discuss what I take to be misunderstandings in Hick's and Palmer's observations. I have not pursued *further* difficulties which arise from what I have said in *The Concept of Prayer*. There *are* such difficulties. For example, consider whether religious language-games could be the *only* language-games played. Could they constitute the whole of a language? If not, why not? This raises interesting and important questions about the relation of religious language-games to *other* language-games. I go on to discuss these questions in the next chapter.

References

1. Hick, John, 'The Justification of Religious Belief'; Palmer, Humphrey, 'Understanding First', *Theology*, lxxi (March 1968). These papers discuss my book, *The Concept of Prayer*.
2. *American Philosophical Quarterly*, i (1964), 309. Reprinted in *Religion and Understanding*, ed. Phillips, D. Z., Basil Blackwell, 1967, 13.
3. *Op. cit.*, 10.
4. 24 n.
5. Winch, Peter, *The Idea of a Social Science*, 101.
6. *Ibid.*, 100.
7. See p. 2.
8. *Ibid.*, 83.
9. *Ibid.*, 84.
10. *Cf.* ch. I, 'Philosophy, Theology, and the Reality of God' in this book (pp. 1–12).

11. *Cf.* Malcolm, Norman, 'Knowledge and Belief' in *Knowledge and Certainty*, Prentice-Hall, 1963.
12. See Wittgenstein, Ludwig, *Lectures and Conversations on Aesthetics, Psychology, and Religious Belief*, Basil Blackwell, 1966, 59.
13. *Ibid.*, 60.
14. Quoted from 'Religion and Epistemology: Some Contemporary Confusions'. See p. 127 of this volume.
15. Pp. 88–95.
16. This really is only an indication of what I have tried to express more fully in chs. 4–6 of *The Concept of Prayer*.
17. *Cf.* Winch, Peter, 'Understanding a Primitive Society', *Religion and Understanding*, 34–8.
18. I repeat this point on p. 83.

V Religious Beliefs and Language-Games

Recently, many philosophers of religion have protested against the philosophical assertion that religious beliefs must be recognized as distinctive language-games. They feel that such an assertion gives the misleading impression that these language-games are cut off from all others. This protest has been made by Ronald Hepburn, John Hick, and Kai Nielsen, to give but three examples. Hepburn says, 'Within traditional Christian theology . . . questions about the divine existence cannot be deflected into the question, "Does 'God' play an intelligible role in the language-game?"'[1] Hick thinks that there is something wrong in saying that 'The logical implications of religious statements do not extend across the border of the *Sprachspiel* into assertions concerning the character of the universe beyond that fragment of it which is the religious speech of human beings.'[2] Nielsen objects to the excessive compartmentalization of modes of social life involved in saying that religious beliefs are distinctive language-games, and argues that 'Religious discourse is not something isolated, sufficient unto itself.[3] Although "Reality" may be systematically ambiguous . . . what constitutes evidence, or tests for the truth or reliability of specific claims, is not completely idiosyncratic to the context or activity we are talking about.

Activities are not that insulated.'[4] I do not want to discuss the writings of these philosophers in this chapter. I have already tried to meet some of their objections elsewhere.[5] Rather, I want to treat their remarks as symptoms of a general misgiving about talking of religious beliefs in the way I have indicated which one comes across with increasing frequency in philosophical writings and in philosophical discussions. I write this chapter as one who has talked of religious beliefs as distinctive language-games, but also as one who has come to feel misgivings in some respects about doing so.

What do these misgivings amount to? Partly, they amount to a feeling that if religious beliefs are isolated, self-sufficient language-games, it becomes difficult to explain why people *should* cherish religious beliefs in the way they do. On the view suggested, religious beliefs seem more like esoteric games, enjoyed by the initiates but of little significance outside the internal formalities of their activities. Religious beliefs begin to look like hobbies – something with which men occupy themselves at week-ends. From other directions, the misgivings involve the suspicion that religious beliefs are being placed outside the reach of any possible criticism, and that the appeal to the internality of religious criteria of meaningfulness can act as a quasi-justification for what would otherwise be recognized as nonsense.

There is little doubt that talk about religious beliefs as distinctive language-games has occasioned these misgivings. As I shall try to show later, to some extent there is good reason for these misgivings. It is also true, however, that these misgivings must be handled with great care. Some attempts at removing them lead to confusions about the logical grammar of certain religious beliefs. In the first two sections of this chapter I shall consider some of these.

I

In face of the misgiving that talk of religious beliefs as distinctive language-games may make them appear to be self-contained esoteric games, some philosophers of religion have denied that such talk is legitimate. What must be established, they argue, is the importance of religious beliefs. People must be given reasons why they ought to believe in God. In this way, religious beliefs are given a basis; they are shown to be reasonable. My difficulty is that I do not understand what is involved in this enterprise.

In his 'Lecture on Ethics', Wittgenstein emphasizes the difference between absolute judgments of value and relative judgments of value. Such words as 'good', 'important', 'right' have a relative and an absolute use. For example, if I say that this is a *good* chair, I may be referring to its adequacy in fulfilling certain purposes. If I say it is *important* not to catch a cold, I may be referring to the unpleasant consequences of doing so. If I say that this is the *right* road, I may be referring to the fact that it would get me to my destination if I follow it.[6] Now, in these instances, I can reverse my judgment as follows: 'This is not a good chair, since I no longer want to relax, but to work.' 'It is not important that I do not catch a cold, since I don't care about the consequences. Doing what I want to do will be worth it.' 'This is not the right road for me, since I no longer want to get to where it would take me.' But as well as a relative use of words like 'good', 'important', 'right', or 'ought', there is an absolute use of the words.

Wittgenstein illustrates the difference where 'ought' is concerned in the following example:

> Supposing that I could play tennis and one of you saw me playing and said, 'Well, you play pretty badly,' and suppose I answered, 'I know I'm playing badly, but I don't want to play any better,' all the other man could say would be: 'Ah, then that's all right.' But suppose I had told one of you a preposterous lie and he came up to me and said, 'You're behaving like a beast,' and then I were to say, 'I know I behave badly, but then I don't want to behave any better,' could he then say, 'Ah, then that's all right'? Certainly not; he would say, 'Well, you *ought* to want to behave better.' Here you have an absolute judgment of value, whereas the first instance was one of a relative judgment.[7]

Many religious apologists feel that if religious beliefs are not to appear as esoteric games they must be shown to be important. This is true as far as it goes. What remains problematic is the way in which the apologists think the importance of religion can be established. When they say it is important to believe in God, how are they using the word 'important'? Are they making a relative or an absolute judgment of value? Sometimes it seems as if relative judgments of value are being made. We are told to believe in God because he is the most powerful being. We are told to believe in God because only those who believe flourish in the end. We are told to believe in God because history is in His hand, and that, despite appearances, the final victory is His. All these advocacies are founded on relative judgments of value. As in the other cases we mentioned, the judgments are reversible. If the Devil happened to be more powerful than God, he would have to be worshipped. If believers are not to flourish in the end, belief becomes pointless. Belief in God is pointless if historical development goes in one direction rather than another.

But need religious beliefs be thought of in this way? Belief in God is represented as a means to a further end. The end is all-important, the means relatively unimportant. Belief in God has a point only if certain consequences follow. This seems to falsify the absolute character which belief in God has for many believers. They would say that God's divinity cannot be justified by external considerations. If we can see nothing in it, there is nothing apart from it which will somehow establish its point. Rush Rhees made a similar observation when he compared an absolute judgment of value in morality with a relative judgment of value:

> 'You ought to make sure that the strip is firmly clamped before you start drilling.' 'What if I don't?' When I tell you what will happen if you don't, you see what I mean.
>
> But 'You ought to want to behave better.' 'What if I don't?' What more could I tell you?[8]

We cannot give a man reasons why he should be good. Similarly, if a man urges someone to come to God, and he asks, 'What if I don't?', what more is there to say? Certainly, one could not get him to believe by telling him that terrible things will happen to him if he does not believe. Even if it were true that these things are going to happen, and even if a person believed because of them, he would not be believing in God. He would be believing in the best thing for himself. He would have

81

a policy, not a faith. Furthermore, if religious beliefs have only a relative value, one can no longer give an account of the distinction between other-worldliness and worldliness, a distinction which is important in most religions. The distinction cannot be accounted for if one assumes that the value of religious beliefs can be assessed by applying them to a wider common measure. Consider the following arguments: (i) We should believe in God. He is the most powerful of all beings. We are all to be judged by Him in the end. He is to determine our fate. In this argument there is only one concept of power: worldly power. *As it happens*, God is more powerful than we are, but it is the same kind of power. (ii) Many battles are fought. At times it looks as if the good is defeated and evil triumphs. But there is no reason to fear: the ultimate victory is God's. Here a common measure is applied to God and the powers of evil, as if God's victory is demonstrable, something recognized by good and evil alike. The man who says God is not victorious would be contradicting the man who says He is victorious.

These apologetic manœuvres remind one of Polus in Plato's *Gorgias*. Polus did not understand Socrates when the latter said that goodness is to a man's advantage. He pointed to Archelaus the Tyrant of Macedonia. Surely, here was a wicked man who flourished. Is it not easy for even a child to show that Socrates is mistaken? But the fallacy in Polus's argument is his supposition that he and Socrates can only mean one thing when they speak of advantage – namely, what he, Polus, means by it. For Socrates, however, it is not the world's view of advantage which is to determine what is good, but what is good which is to determine what is to count as advantage. In what way are some apologists similar to Polus? In this way: when someone shows them how much power the forces ranged against religion have, they reply, 'But our God is more powerful!' But they use the same concept of power. Their idea of power is not qualitatively different from that of their opponents. On the contrary, on their view the world and God share the same kind of power, only God has more of it. But, like Polus, they need to realize that for many believers it is not the outcome, the course of events, which is to determine whether God is victorious, but faith in God which determines what is regarded as victory. If this were not so, there would be no tension between the world's ways of regarding matters and religious reactions to them. The same tension exists in ethics. There are those for whom justice, to be worth pursuing, must be acceptable to a thousand tough characters. Others, like Socrates, recognizing that in Athens or any other city anything may happen to one, can say without contradiction that all will be well. In the eyes of the world, all cannot be well if anything will happen to one. Things must go in one way rather than another. Since, for many believers, love of God determines what is to count as important, there will be situations where what the believer calls 'success' will be failure in the eyes of the world, what he calls 'joy' will seem like grief, what he calls 'victory' will seem like certain defeat. So it was, Christians believe, at the Cross of Christ.[9] In drawing attention to this tension between two points of view, my aim is not to advocate either, but to show that any account of religious beliefs which seems to deny that such a tension exists falsifies the nature of the beliefs in question.

What we have seen in the first section of the chapter is how, if philosophers are not careful, misgivings about treating religious beliefs as esoteric games can lead to an attempt to show why religious beliefs are important which distorts the nature of the values involved in such beliefs.

II

Misgivings about the philosophical characterization of religious beliefs as distinctive language-games not only lead to attempts to give an external justification of religious values, but also to attempts both by philosophers who are sympathetic and by philosophers who are unsympathetic to religion to show that their conclusions are reached by criteria of rationality which their opponents do or ought to accept. Unless believers and non-believers can be shown to be using common criteria of rationality, it is said, then the misgivings about religious beliefs being esoteric games cannot be avoided.

Wittgenstein raised the question whether, in relation to religion, the non-believer contradicts the believer when he says that he does not believe what the believer believes.[10] If one man contradicts another, they can be said to share a common understanding, to be playing the same game. Consider the following examples: The man who says that the sun is 90 million miles away from the earth contradicts the man who says that the sun is only 20 million miles away from the earth. The man who says that the profit from a business venture is £100,000 is contradicted by the man who says that the profit is £50,000. The man who says that there are unicorns contradicts the man who says that there are no unicorns. In these examples the disputants participate in a common understanding. The disputants about the distance of the sun from the earth share a common understanding – namely, methods of calculation in astronomy. The disputants about the business profit share a common understanding – namely, business methods of calculating gain and loss. The disputants about the unicorns share a common understanding – namely, methods of verifying the existence of various kinds of animals. The disputants differ about the facts, but they are one in logic – that is, they appeal to the same criteria to settle the disagreement. But what if one man says that handling the ball is a foul and another says that handling the ball is not a foul? Are they contradicting each other? Surely they are only doing so if they are playing the same game, referring to the same rules.

In the light of these examples, what are we to say about the man who believes in God and the man who does not? Are they contradicting each other? Are two people, one of whom says there is a God and the other of whom says he does not believe in God, like two people who disagree about the existence of unicorns? Wittgenstein shows that they are not.[11] The main reason for the difference is that God's reality is not one of a kind; He is not a being among beings. The word 'God' is not the name of a thing. Thus, the reality of God cannot be assessed by a common measure which also applies to things other than God. But these are conclusions for which reasons must be given.

If I say that something exists, it makes sense to think of that something ceasing to exist. But religious believers do not want to say that God might cease to exist. This is not because, as a matter of fact, they think God will exist for ever, but because it is meaningless to speak of God's ceasing to exist. Again, we cannot ask of God the kinds of questions we can ask of things which come to be and pass away: 'What brought Him into existence?' 'When will He cease to exist?' 'He was existing yesterday. How about today?' Again, we find religious believers saying that it is a terrible thing not to believe in God. But if believing in God is to believe in the existence of a thing, an object, one might wonder why it is so terrible to say that the thing in question does not exist.[12] Or one might be puzzled as to why there is such a fuss about these matters, anyway, since religious believers only *believe* them to be true. We might say, as we would normally in such cases, 'You only believe – Oh, well . . .'[11] But is this the way in which the word 'belief' is used in religion? Is it not queer to say of worshippers, 'They only believe there is a God'?

What is the reaction of philosophers to these differences? They are not unaware of them. On the contrary, we have quarterly reminders of their multiplicity. But most philosophers who write on the subject see these differences as an indication that serious blunders have been committed in the name of religion for some reason or another. Once the differences are seen as blunders, it is assumed that what are sometimes called 'the logical peculiarities' of religious discourse are deviations from or distortions of non-religious ways of speaking with which we are familiar. Thus, the reality of God is made subject to wider criteria of intelligibility. Like the particular hypotheses about the distance of the sun from the earth, the profit in business, or the existence of unicorns, beliefs about God are thought to have a relative reality – that is, the reality of a hypothesis which is relative to the criteria by which it is assessed. In the case of religious beliefs, it is said that when they are brought into relation with the relevant criteria of assessment they are shown to be mistakes, distortions, illusions, or blunders. If I understand Wittgenstein, he is saying that this conclusion arises, partly at least, from a deep philosophical prejudice. One characteristic of this prejudice is the craving for generality, the insistence that what constitutes an intelligible move in one context must constitute an intelligible move in all contexts. The insistence, to take our examples, that the use of 'existence' and 'belief' is the same in all contexts, and the failure to recognize this as an illegitimate elevation of *one* use of these words as a paradigm for *any* use of the words. What Wittgenstein shows us in his remarks on religious belief is why there is good reason to note the different uses which 'belief' and 'existence' have, and to resist the craving for generality.

One of the ways of generalizing which has serious implications, and leads to a host of misunderstandings in philosophical discussions of religion, is to think that nothing can be believed unless there is evidence or grounds for that belief. Of course, where certain religious beliefs are concerned – for example, belief in the authenticity of a holy relic – grounds and evidence for the belief are relevant. But one cannot conclude that it makes sense to ask for the evidence or grounds of every religious belief. Wittgenstein considers belief in the Last Judgment. Now, one way of proceeding is to ask what evidence there is for believing in the Last Judgment. One could imagine degrees of belief concerning it: some say they are sure about it, others say that possibly there will be a Last Judgment, others do not believe in it. But, despite these disagreements, we can say, as we did of our earlier examples, that the disputants are one in logic. The Last Judgment seems to be thought of as a future event which may or may not occur. Those who feel sure it will occur, those who think it might possibly occur, and those who do not think it will occur are all, logically, on the same level. They are all playing the same game: they are expressing their belief, half-belief, or unbelief in a hypothesis. So this religious belief is taken to be a hypothesis.

But need religious beliefs always be hypotheses? Clearly not. Wittgenstein points out that the word 'God' is amongst the earliest learnt. We learn it through pictures, stories, catechisms, etc. But, Wittgenstein warns us, this does not have 'the same consequences as with pictures of aunts. I wasn't shown (that which the picture pictured).'[13] Later, Wittgenstein illustrates the point as follows:

Take 'God created man'. Pictures of Michelangelo showing the creation of the world. In general, there is nothing which explains the meanings of words as well as a picture, and I take it that Michelangelo was as good as anyone can be and did his best, and here is the picture of the Deity creating Adam.

If we ever saw this, we certainly wouldn't think this the Deity. The picture has to be used in an entirely different way if we are to call the man in that queer blanket 'God', and so on. You could imagine that religion was taught by means of these pictures. 'Of course we can only express ourselves by means of pictures.' This is rather queer. . . . I could show

Moore the pictures of a tropical plant. There is a technique of comparison between picture and plant. If I showed him the picture of Michelangelo and said, 'Of course, I can't show you the real thing, only the picture' . . . The absurdity is, I've never taught him the technique of using this picture.[14]

So the difference between a man who does and a man who does not believe in God is like the difference between a man who does and a man who does not believe in a picture. But what does believing in a picture amount to? Is it like believing in a hypothesis? Certainly not. As Wittgenstein says, 'The whole *weight* may be in the picture.'[15] A man's belief in the Last Judgment may show itself in a way a man has this before his mind when he takes any decisions of importance, in the way it determines his attitude to his aspirations and failures, or to the fortunes or misfortunes which befall him. In referring to these features of the religious person's beliefs, Wittgenstein is stressing the grammar of belief in this context. He is bringing out what 'recognition of a belief' amounts to here. It does not involve the weighing of evidence or reasoning to a conclusion. What it does involve is seeing how the belief regulates a person's life. 'Here believing obviously plays much more this role: suppose we said that a certain picture might play the role of constantly admonishing me, or I always think of it. Here an enormous difference would be between those people for whom the picture is constantly in the foreground, and the others who just didn't use it at all.'[16] What, then, are we to say of those who do not use the picture, who do not believe in it? Do they contradict those who do? Wittgenstein shows that they do not:

Suppose someone is ill and he says: 'This is a punishment', and I say: 'If I'm ill, I don't think of punishment at all.' If you say, 'Do you believe the opposite?' – you can call it believing the opposite, but it is entirely different from what we would normally call believing the opposite.

I think differently, in a different way. I say different things to myself. I have different pictures.

It is this way: if someone said, 'Wittgenstein, you don't take illness as punishment, so what do you believe?' – I'd say: 'I don't have any thoughts of punishment.'[17]

Those who do not use the picture cannot be compared, therefore, with those who do not believe in a hypothesis. Believing in the picture means, for example, putting one's trust in it, sacrificing for it, letting it regulate one's life, and so on. Not believing in the picture means that the picture plays no part in one's thinking. Wittgenstein brings out the difference between this and disputants over a hypothesis very neatly when he says, 'Suppose someone were a believer and said: "I believe in a Last Judgment," and I said: "Well, I'm not so sure. Possibly." You would say that there is an enormous gulf between us. If he said "There is a German aeroplane overhead," and I said "Possibly. I'm not so sure," you'd say we were fairly near.'[18]

Beliefs, such as belief in the Last Judgment, are not testable hypotheses, but absolutes for believers in so far as they predominate in and determine much of their thinking. The absolute beliefs are the criteria, not the object of assessment. To construe these beliefs as hypotheses which may or may not be true is to falsify their character. As Wittgenstein says: 'The point is that if there were evidence, this would in fact destroy the whole business.'[19] The difficulty is in seeing what might be meant in saying that absolute religious beliefs could turn out to be mistakes or blunders. As Wittgenstein points out, 'Whether a thing is a blunder or not – it is a blunder in a particular system. Just as something is a blunder in a particular game and not in another.'[20] Some blunders may be pretty fundamental. Others may be elementary. We can see what has gone wrong if, when asked to go on in the same way, someone continues the series 2, 4, 6, 8, 10 . . . by repeating it. But, Wittgenstein says, 'If you suddenly wrote numbers down on the blackboard, and then said, "Now, I'm going to add," and then said, "2 and 21 is 13," etc., I'd say: "This is no blunder".'[21] We do not say that the person has made a blunder in adding. We say that he is not adding at all. We may say that he is fooling, or that he is insane. Consider now the view that evidence for religious beliefs is very slender. Wittgenstein considers the example of a man who dreams of the Last Judgment and then says he knows what it must be like.[22] If we think of this as we think of attempts to assess next week's weather, it is queer to think of the dream as slender evidence. 'If you compare it with anything in science which we call evidence, you can't credit that anyone could soberly argue: "Well, I had this dream . . . therefore . . . Last Judgment." You might say, "For a blunder, that's too big." '[23] As in the other case, you might look for other explanations. You might say that the believer is joking or insane. But this brings us precisely to the heart of the misgivings I mentioned at the outset. How do we know that religious practices aren't forms of disguised nonsense which, for some reason or another, believers do not recognize as such? This question brings us to the final section of the chapter.

III

So far I have been stressing how certain philosophers, because they have feared the implications of describing religious beliefs as distinctive language-games, have tried to show why religious beliefs are important in much the same way as one might show a certain course of action to be prudential; or have tried to show the rationality of religious beliefs by assuming that the existence of God is to be established by reference to criteria under which it falls as *one* appropriate instance among many. Such attempts, I argued, falsify the absolute character of many religious beliefs and values.

Against this it might be urged that, on my view, religious believers can say what they like. Such a reaction is strengthened when philosophers talk of language-games as having criteria of intelligibility within them, and of the impossibility of rendering one language-game unintelligible in terms of criteria of intelligibility taken from another. It is important, however, not to confuse the view I have argued for with another which has superficial resemblances to it. The view I have in mind was once put forward by T. H. McPherson: 'Religion belongs to the sphere of the unsayable, so it is not to be wondered at that in theology there is much nonsense (i.e. many absurdities); this is the natural result of trying to put into words – and to discuss – various kinds of inexpressible "experiences", and of trying to say things about God.'[24] J. A. Passmore comments on this observation: 'One difficulty with this line of reasoning, considered as a defence of religion, is that it "saves" religion only at the cost of leaving the door open to any sort of transcendental metaphysics – and indeed to superstition and nonsense of the most arrant sort.'[25] One difference between calling religious beliefs distinctive language-games and McPherson's observations is that there is no talk of incomprehensibility in the former. On the contrary, within religious practices there will be criteria for what can and cannot be said. So a believer can commit blunders within his religion. But this observation might not satisfy the critics, since they might argue that a set of pointless rules could have an internal consistency. People can follow, and therefore fail to follow, pointless rules. In that way they may make mistakes. But the possibility of their being correct or incorrect would not of itself confer a point on a set of pointless rules. To argue, therefore, that religious beliefs are distinctive language-games with rules which their adherents may follow or fail to follow does not, of itself, show that the rules have any point.

I think the misgivings I have outlined are justified. They point to a strain in the analogy between religious beliefs as games. The point of religious beliefs, why people *should* cherish them in the way they do, cannot be shown simply by *distinguishing between* religious beliefs and other features of human existence. What I am saying is that the importance of religion in people's lives cannot be understood simply by distinguishing between religion and other modes of social life, although, as we have seen, there are important distinctions to be made in this way. I had said elsewhere that if religion were thought of as cut off from other modes of social life it could not have the importance it has, but I had not realized the full implications of these remarks.[26] I have been helped to see them more clearly by Rush Rhees's important paper, 'Wittgenstein's Builders'.[27]

In the *Tractatus* Wittgenstein thought that all propositions must, simply by being propositions, have a general form. Rhees says that, although Wittgenstein had given up the idea of 'all propositions' in the *Investigations*, he was still interested in human language and in what belonging to a common language meant:

> When he says that any language is a family of language-games, and that any of these might be a complete language by itself, he does not say whether people who might take part in several such games would be speaking the same language in each of them. In fact, I find it hard to see on this view that they would *ever* be speaking a language.[28]

Why does Rhees say this? One important reason, as he says, is that Wittgenstein takes it for granted that the same language is being spoken in the different language-games. But if this is so the sameness or unity of that language cannot be explained by describing the way in which any *particular* language-game is played. The problem becomes acute when Wittgenstein says that each language-game could be a complete language in itself. One reason why Wittgenstein said that each language-game is complete is that he wanted to rid us of the supposition that all propositions have a general form. The different language-games do not make up one big game. For the most part, this is what I have been stressing in relation to religious language-games in this chapter, but it gives rise to new problems. The different games do not make up a game, and yet Wittgenstein wants to say that a language, the same language, *is* a family of language-games – that is, that this is the kind of unity a language has. At this point there is a strain in the analogy between language and a game.

In the example of the builders at the beginning of the *Investigations*, Wittgenstein says that the language of orders and response, one man shouting 'Slab!' and another bringing one, could be the entire language of a tribe. Rhees says: 'But I feel that there is something wrong here. The trouble is not to imagine a people with a language of such limited vocabulary. The trouble is to imagine that they spoke the language only to give these special orders on this job and otherwise never spoke at all. I do not think it would be speaking a language.'[29]

As Rhees points out, Wittgenstein imagines the children of the tribe being taught these shouts by adults. But such teaching would not be part of the technique of order and response on the actual job. Presumably, men go home and sometimes discuss their work with their families. Sometimes one has to discuss snags which crop up in the course of a job. Those things are not part of a technique either. What Wittgenstein describes, Rhees argues, is more like a game with building stones and the correct methods of reacting to signals than people actually building a house. What Rhees is stressing is that learning a language cannot be equated with learning what is generally done: 'It has more to do with what it makes sense to answer or what it makes sense to ask, or what sense one remark may have in connection with another.'[30] The expressions used by the builders cannot have their meaning entirely within the job. We would not be able to grasp the meaning of expressions, see the bearing of one expression on another, appreciate why something can be said here but not there, unless expressions were connected with contexts other than those in which we are using them now. Rhees says that when a child comes to learn the differences between sensible discourse and a jumble of words, this

> is not something you can teach him by any sort of drill, as you might perhaps teach him the names of objects. I think he gets it chiefly from the way in which the members of his family speak to him and answer him. In this way he gets an idea of how remarks may be connected, and of how what people say to one another makes sense. In any case, it is not like learning the meaning of this or that expression. And although he can go on speaking, this is not like going on with the use of any particular expression or set of expressions, although of course it includes that.[31]

What Rhees says of the builders can also be said of worshippers. If the orders and responses of the builders are cut off from everything outside the technique on the job, we seem to be talking about a game with building blocks, a system of responses to signs, rather than about the building of an actual house. Similarly, if we think of religious worship as cut off from everything outside the formalities of worship, it ceases to be worship and becomes an esoteric game. What is the difference between a rehearsal for an act of worship and the actual act of worship? The answer cannot be in terms of responses to signs, since the responses to signs may be correct in the rehearsal. The difference has to do with the point the activity has in the life of the worshippers, the bearing it has on other features of their lives. Religion has something to say about aspects of human existence which are quite intelligible without reference to religion: birth, death, joy, misery, despair, hope, fortune and misfortune. The connection between these and religion is not contingent. A host of religious beliefs could not be what they are without them. The force of religious beliefs depends, in part, on what is outside religion. Consider, for example, Jesus's words, 'Not as the world giveth give I unto you.' Here the force of the contrast between the teaching of Jesus and worldliness depends, logically, on both parts of the contrast. One could not understand the sense in which Jesus gives unless one also understands the sense in which the world gives. So far from it being true that religious beliefs can be thought of as isolated language-games, cut off from all other forms of life, the fact is that religious beliefs cannot be understood at all unless their relation to other forms of life is taken into account. Suppose someone were to object to this, 'No. What you need to understand is religious language,' what would one think of it? One could not be blamed if it reminded one of those who think that all will be well if an acceptable liturgy is devised – a piece of empty aestheticism. Religion could then be described literally as a game, a neat set of rules with ever-increasing refinements in their interpretation and execution. It would be impossible to distinguish between genuine and sham worship. As long as the moves and responses in the liturgical game were correct, nothing more could be said. In fact, we should have described what religious practices often do become for those for whom they have lost their meaning: a charming game which provides a welcome contrast to the daily routine, but which has no relevance to anything outside the doors of the church. I suppose that Father Sergius knew more about religious language, the formalities of worship, than Pashenka. She was so absorbed in her day-to-day duties in cleaning the church that she never had time to read the Bible herself or to attend worship. But her devotion, sacrifice and humility were such that Sergius was led to say that she lived for God and imagined she lived for men, while he, versed in religious rite and language, lived for men and imagined he lived for God.

Religion must take the world seriously. I have argued that religious reactions to various situations cannot be assessed according to some external criteria of adequacy. On the other hand, the connections between religious beliefs and such situations must not be fantastic. This in no way contradicts the earlier arguments, since whether the connections are fantastic is decided by criteria which are not in dispute. For example, some religious believers may try to explain away the reality of suffering, or try to say that all suffering has some purpose. When they speak like this, one may accuse them of not taking suffering seriously. Or if religious believers talk of death as if it were a sleep of long duration, one may accuse them of not taking death seriously. In these examples, what is said about suffering and death can be judged in terms of what we already know and believe about these matters. The religious responses are fantastic because they ignore or distort what we already know. What is said falls under standards of judgment with which we are already acquainted. When what is said by religious believers does violate the facts or distort our apprehension of situations, no appeal to the fact that what is said is said in the name of religion can justify or excuse the violation and distortion.

Furthermore, one must stress the connection between religious beliefs and the world, not only in bringing out the force which these beliefs have, but also in bringing out the nature of the difficulties which the beliefs may occasion. If religious beliefs were isolated language-games, cut off from everything which is not formally religious, how could there be any of the characteristic difficulties connected with religious beliefs? The only difficulties which could arise would be akin to the difficulties connected with mastering a complex technique. But these are not the kind of difficulties which do arise in connection with religious beliefs. Is not *striving* to believe itself an important feature of religious belief? Why should this be so?

Consider, for example, difficulties which arise because of a tension between a believer's beliefs and his desires. He may find it difficult to overcome his pride, his envy, or his lust. But these difficulties cannot be understood unless serious account is taken of what pride, envy, and lust involve. Neither can the positive virtues be understood without reference to the vices to which they are contrasted.

Consider also difficulties of another kind, not difficulties in holding to one's beliefs in face of temptation, but difficulties in believing. The problem of evil occasions the most well-known of these. One might have heard someone talk of what it means to accept a tragedy as the will of God. He might have explained what Jesus meant when He said that a man must be prepared to leave his father and mother for His sake by pointing out that this does not imply that children should forsake their parents. What Jesus was trying to show, he might say, is that for the believer the death of a loved one must not make life meaningless. If it did, he would have given the loved one a place in his life which should only be given to God. The believer must be able to leave his father and mother – that is, face parting with them – and still be able to find the meaning of his life in God. Listening to this exposition, one might have thought it expressed what one's own beliefs amounted to. But then, suddenly, one has to face the death of one's child, and one realizes that one cannot put into practice, or find any strength or comfort in, the beliefs one had said were one's own. The untimely death of one's child renders talk of God's love meaningless for one. One might want to believe, but one simply cannot. This is not because a hypothesis has been assessed or a theory tested, and found wanting. It would be nearer the truth to say that a person cannot bring himself to react in a certain way; he has no use for a certain picture of the situation. The point I wish to stress, however, is that no sense can be made of this difficulty unless due account is taken of the tragedy. If religion were an esoteric game, why should the tragedy have any bearing on it at all? Why should the tragedy be a difficulty for faith or a trial of faith?

From the examples considered, it can be seen that the meaning and force of religious beliefs depend in part on the relation of these beliefs to features of human existence other than religion. Without such dependence, religion would not have the importance it does have in people's lives. It is an awareness of these important truths which in part accounts for the philosophical objections to talking of religious beliefs as distinctive language-games. But these objections are confused, the result of drawing false conclusions from important truths. Having recognized, correctly, that the meaning of religious beliefs is partly dependent on features of human life outside religion, philosophers conclude, wrongly, that one would be contradicting oneself if one claimed to recognize this dependence, and also claimed that religious beliefs are distinctive language-games. They are led to this conclusion *only because they assume that the relation between religious beliefs and the non-religious facts is that between what is justified and its justification, or that between a conclusion and its grounds.* This is a far-reaching confusion. To say that the meaning of religious beliefs is partly dependent on non-religious facts is not to say that those beliefs are justified by, or could be inferred from, the facts in question.

The main points I have been trying to emphasize in this chapter can be summed up in terms of some examples:

A boxer crosses himself before the fight; a mother places a garland on a statue of the Virgin Mary; parents pray for their child lost in a wreck. Are these blunders or religious activities? What decides the answer to this question is the surroundings, what the people involved say about their actions, what their expectations are, what, if anything, would render the activity pointless, and so on. Does the boxer think that anyone who crosses himself before a fight will not come to serious harm in it? Does the mother think that the garland's value is prudential? Do the parents believe that all true prayers for the recovery of children lead to that recovery? If these questions are answered in the affirmative, the beliefs involved become testable hypotheses. They are, as a matter of fact, blunders, mistakes, regarding causal connections of a kind. We can say that the people involved are reasoning wrongly, meaning by this that they contradict what we already know. The activities are brought under a system where theory, repeatability, explanatory force, etc., are important features, and they are shown to be wanting, shown to be blunders. But perhaps the activities have a different meaning. Perhaps the boxer is dedicating his performance in crossing himself, expressing the hope that it be worthy of what he believes in, and so on. The mother may be venerating the birth of her child as God's gift, thanking for it, and contemplating the virtues of motherhood as found in the mother of Jesus. The parents may be making their desires known to God, wanting the situation which has occasioned them to be met in Him. The beliefs involved are not testable hypotheses, but ways of reacting to and meeting such situations. They are expressions of faith and trust. Not to use these objects of faith, not to have any time for the reactions involved, is not to believe. The distinction between religious belief and superstition is extremely important. I want to emphasize it by considering one of the above examples in a little more detail.

Consider again the example of two mothers who ask the Virgin Mary to protect their newly-born babies. Tylor would say that this is an example of 'a blind belief in processes wholly irrelevant to their supposed results'.[32] What I am stressing is that such a description begs the question as to what is meant by 'belief', 'processes', 'relevance', and 'results' in this context. For Tylor the supposed results would be the future material welfare of the child, and the irrelevant processes would be the bringing of the child to a statue of the Virgin Mary and the connections which might be thought to exist between this and the future fortunes of the child. How could the irrelevance be demonstrated? The answer seems to be simple. All one needs is a comparison of the material fortunes of babies for whom the blessing of the Virgin has been sought and the material fortunes of those who have received no such blessing. The results will be statistically random. One is reminded of the suggestion that the efficacy of prayer could be shown by observations of two patients suffering from the same ailment, one of whom is treated medically and the other of whom is simply prayed for. The idea seems to be that prayer is a way of getting things done which competes with other ways of getting things done, and that the superiority of one way over the other could be settled experimentally. Now, of course, I am not denying that a mother who brings her baby to the Virgin Mary could have the kind of expectations which Tylor would attribute to *any* mother who asks the Virgin to protect her baby. And I agree that, if these were her expectations, her act would be a superstitious one. What characterizes the superstitious act in this context? Firstly, there is the trust in non-existent, quasi-causal connections: the belief that someone long dead called the Virgin Mary can, if she so desires, determine the course of an individual's life, keep him from harm, make his ventures succeed, and so on. Secondly, the Virgin Mary is seen as a means to ends which are intelligible without reference to her: freedom from harm, successful ventures, etc. In other words, the act of homage to the Virgin Mary has no importance in itself;

she is reduced to the status of a lucky charm. What one *says* to the Virgin makes no difference. But someone may object to this. How can this be said? Surely what is said to her makes all the difference in the world. If one worships before her one is blessed with good fortune, but if one blasphemes one is cursed with bad fortune. But this is precisely why I say that what one says to the Virgin makes no difference. *As it happens*, freedom from physical harm, fortune in one's ventures, are secured in this way, but the way is only important in so far as these things are secured. If they could be obtained more economically or more abundantly by pursuing some other way, that way would be adopted. What is said is only important as long as it leads to the desired end, *an end which can be understood independently of what is said.* On this view, the act of bringing one's child to the Virgin could be shown to be valid or invalid in terms of future consequences.

But why is it confused to understand *all* acts of homage to the Virgin in this way? The answer is: because the religious character of the homage paid to the Virgin is completely ignored. Or, at least, it is assumed that its religious character is reducible to its efficacy *as one way among others* of securing certain ends. As I have said, bringing a child to a statue of the Virgin may be superstitious, but it may not. A mother may bring her new-born baby to the mother of Jesus in an act of veneration and thanksgiving; one mother greets another at the birth of a child. Connected with this act of greeting are a number of associated beliefs and attitudes: wonder and gratitude in face of new life, humility at being the means of bringing a child into the world, and, in this case, recognition of life as God's gift, the givenness of life. But what about the protection sought for the child? What is important to recognize is that the protection must be understood in terms of these beliefs and attitudes. These virtues and attitudes are all contained in the person of Mary, the mother of Jesus. For the believer she is the paradigm of these virtues and attitudes. They constitute her holiness. Now, when her protection is sought, the protection is the protection of her holiness: the mother wants the child's life to be orientated in these virtues. The first act in securing such an orientation is the bringing of the child to the Virgin. This orientation is what the believer would call the blessing of the Virgin Mary.

The difference between the two situations I want to contrast should now be clear. In the one case, the protection determines whether or not the act of bringing the child to the Virgin and the alleged holiness of the Virgin have been efficacious or not. In the other case, it is the holiness of the Virgin which determines the nature of the protection. In Tylor's account there is no need to refer to the religious significance which the Virgin Mary has for believers. But, on the view I am urging, you cannot understand the request for a blessing unless that is taken account of, or think of the blessing as one way among many of producing the same result.

The above remarks can be applied to one of Tylor's own examples. Tylor believes that the soul is migrant, 'capable of leaving the body far behind, to flash swiftly from place to place'.[33] He traces among various peoples the belief in the soul as breath or a ghost:

And if any should think such expression due to mere metaphor, they may judge the strength of the implied connection between breath and spirit by cases of most unequivocal significance. Among the Seminoles of Florida, when a woman died in childbirth the infant was held over her face to receive her parting spirit, and thus acquire strength and knowledge for its future use. These Indians could have well understood why at the death-bed of an ancient Roman the nearest kinsman leant over to inhale the last breath of the departing. . . . Their state of mind is kept up to this day among Tyrolese peasants, who can still fancy a good man's soul to issue from his mouth at death like a little white cloud.[34]

Tylor thinks that the meaning of these examples is unequivocal: power is being transferred from one being to another by means of the transfer of a soul which he envisages as a non-material substance. Notice the neglect of the situations in which these actions take place. All Tylor sees is the alleged transfer of pseudo-power by odd means. If we asked Tylor why the mother's soul *should* be transferred to the baby rather than to anyone else, or why the ancient Roman's soul *should* be transferred to the nearst kinsman rather than to anyone else, I suppose he would answer that such a transfer was laid down by social rules. He might even say that such a transfer is natural. But the naturalness is not brought out at all by Tylor's analysis. On his view, the power, via the migrant soul, could have gone into *any* being, but as it happened it was decreed or thought natural that it should go where it did.

We get a very different picture if we take note of the situations in which these actions take place: the relationship between a dying mother and her child and the relationship between a dying man and his nearest kinsman. In these cases, why should Tylor find the symbolic actions odd? A mother has given her life in bringing her child into the world. The breath of life, her mother's life, her mother's soul, is breathed into the child. Surely this is an act of great beauty. But one cannot understand it outside the relationship between a dying mother and her child. Similarly, it is in terms of the relationship between a dying man and his next of kin that the symbolic act of passing on authority and tradition is to be understood. It would not make sense to say that *anyone* could be the object of these acts. If the wrong child were held over the dying woman's face, what would be terrible is not, as Tylor thinks, that power has been transferred to the wrong person, but that this child hasn't the relationship to the woman that her own child has: it is not the child for whom she gave her life. The expression of love and sacrifice expressed in the mother's parting breath is violated if it is received by the wrong child.

In the examples we have considered we have seen that the religious or ritualistic practices could not be what they are were it not for factors independent of them. The internal consistency of rules, something to which astrology could appeal, does not show that the rules have a point. To see this one must take account of the connection between the practices and other features of the lives people lead. It is such connections which enable us to see that astrology is superstitious and that many religious practices can be distinguished from superstition, while other so-called religious practices turn out to be superstitious.

But the main point I wish to stress is that it does not

make sense to ask for a proof of the validity of religious beliefs, whatever that might mean. Consider, finally, the example of the mother who reacts to the birth of her baby by an act of devotion to the Virgin Mary. It is true that the act of devotion could not be what it is without the birth of the baby, which, after all, occasioned it. It is also true that the connection between the religious act and the baby's birth must not be fantastic.[35] It must be shown not to be superstition. But having made these points, it is also important to stress that the birth is not evidence from which one can assess the religious reaction to it. People react to the birth of children in various ways. Some may say that the birth of a child is always a cause for rejoicing. Others may say that whether one rejoices at the birth of a child should be determined by the physical and mental health of the child, or by whether the family into which it is born can look after it properly. Others may say that one should always give thanks to God when a child is born. Others may condemn the folly of those responsible for bringing a child into a world such as this. All these reactions are reactions to the birth of a child, and could not mean what they do apart from the fact of the birth. But it does not follow that the various reactions can be inferred from the birth, or that they are conclusions for which the birth of the baby is the ground. All one can say is that people *do* respond in this way. Many who respond in one way will find the other responses shallow, trivial, fantastic, meaningless, or even evil. But the force of the responses cannot be justified in any external way; it can merely be shown. This is true of religious responses, the religious beliefs which have an absolute character and value. Philosophy may clarify certain misunderstandings about them. It may show the naïvety of certain objections to religion, or that some so-called religious beliefs are superstitions. But philosophy is neither for nor against religious beliefs. After it has sought to clarify the grammar of such beliefs its work is over. As a result of such clarification, someone may see dimly that religious beliefs are not what he had taken them to be. He may stop objecting to them, even though he does not believe in them. Someone else may find that now he is able to believe. Another person may hate religion more than he did before the philosophical clarification. The results are unpredictable. In any case, they are not the business of philosophy.

References

1. Hepburn, R. W., 'From World to God', *Mind*, lxxii (1963), 41.
2. Hick, John, 'Sceptics and Believers' in *Faith and the Philosophers*, ed. Hick, J., Macmillan, 1964, 239.
3. Nielsen, Kai 'Wittgensteinian Fideism' in *Philosophy*, July 1967, 207.
4. *Ibid.*, p. 208.
5. See ch. VII, pp. 123–45.
6. See Wittgenstein, Ludwig, 'A Lecture on Ethics', *Philosophical Review*, January 1965, 8.
7. *Ibid.*, 5.
8. Rhees, Rush, 'Some Developments in Wittengstein's View of Ethics', *Philosophical Review*, January 1965, pp. 18–19.
9. See p. 75.
10. Wittgenstein, Ludwig, *Lectures and Conversations on Aesthetics, Psychology, and Religious Belief*, ed. Barrett, Cyril, Basil Blackwell, 1966, 53–72. The lectures are selections from notes taken by

Wittgenstein's students. They do not claim to be a verbatim report of his words.

11. I have tried to argue for a similar conclusion in *The Concept of Prayer*, Routledge & Kegan Paul, 1965. See chs. 1 and 2.

12. Wittgenstein's examples. See *op. cit.*, 59–60.

13. *Ibid.*, 59.

14. *Ibid.*, 63.

15. *Ibid.*, 72.

16. *Ibid.*, 56.

17. *Ibid.*, 55.

18. *Ibid.*, 53.

19. *Ibid.*, 56.

20. *Ibid.*, 59.

21. *Ibid.*, 62.

22. See *ibid.*, 61.

23. *Ibid.*, 61–2.

24. McPherson, T. H., 'Religion as the Inexpressible' in *New Essays in Philosophical Theology*, ed. Flew, A., and MacIntyre, A., S.C.M. Press, 1955, 142.

25. Passmore, J. A., 'Christianity and Positivism' in the *Australasian Journal of Philosophy*, xxxv (1957), 128.

26. *Cf.* pp. 9, 21, 230–1 of this volume.

27. Rhees, R., 'Wittgenstein's Builders', *Proceedings of the Aristotelian Society*, 1959–60; reprinted in *Ludwig Wittgenstein: the Man and His Philosophy*, ed. Fann, K. T., Delta Books, 1967, and Rhees, R., *Discussions of Wittgenstein*, Routledge & Kegan Paul, 1970.

28. *Ibid.*, 253.

29. *Ibid.*, 256.

30. *Ibid.*, 260.

31. *Ibid.*, 262.

32. *Primitive Culture*, i. 133.

33. *Ibid.*, i, xi. 429.

34. *Ibid.*, 433.

35. Of course, the matter may be further complicated by the fact that people may well disagree over whether a given 'connection' is fantastic or not.

VI Belief and Loss of Belief

(*A Discussion with J. R. Jones*[1])

D.Z.P.: Jargon is the enemy of philosophy. It creates
a screen between the enquirer and the possibility of
understanding. Furthermore, if a certain jargon has
become a prevalent fashion in philosophical circles,
using it, and hearing it used, may lead a person to think
he has understood, when, in fact, he has not. There is a
great need to cut through some prevalent jargon in contemporary philosophy of religion. We need to be forced
to see that many religious beliefs cannot be understood
in terms of the neat categories which, we are tempted to
think, are the only categories which intelligible notions
have. For example, in his lectures on religious belief,[2]
Wittgenstein considers religious beliefs like belief in the
Last Judgment, or that one's life is being lived under
the eye of God. We cannot grasp the nature of these
beliefs by forcing them into the alternatives: empirical
propositions or human attitudes. And yet, again and
again, philosophers of religion force our hands by saying, 'But come now, which is it? Is the Last Judgment a
future event? Is it something which is going to happen
at a certain time? Or is belief in the Last Judgment
simply your own attitude, a value, a way of looking at
things, which you confer on the world about you?'
What Wittgenstein does is to free us from this jargon. It
is as if he said to us, 'Don't say it *must* be one or the

other. Look and see what kind of things these beliefs are. Don't let the jargon determine your thinking.' Or, as Wittgenstein used to say, 'Don't think, look.' Don't say that religious beliefs *must* be of this kind or that, but look to see what kind of beliefs they are. And when we do this, Wittgenstein suggests, we stop asking many questions of religious belief which, before, we thought it quite reasonable to ask. For example, we stop thinking of religious beliefs as conjectures, hypotheses, for which the evidence is not particularly good. In the light of our reflections on religious beliefs, we may be led to revise our opinions about the distinction between the rational and the irrational, and to think again about what might be meant by saying that one does not have any religious beliefs. What does it mean to believe in the Last Judgment? What does it mean to say that one does not believe in it? Must we say one or the other, or is this a mistake we are led into because of the hold of a certain jargon on us? These are some of the questions Professor Jones and I are going to try to discuss. We do no more than touch lightly on them. At this stage, all we are attempting to do is to indicate a direction in which these questions can be pursued with profit.

J.R.J.: I should like to draw you out first, Mr Phillips, on the point that religious belief is nothing like the acceptance of a hypothesis or the holding of an opinion, however well- or ill-founded. I wonder whether this can be seen to be so by just looking at the role beliefs have in the believers' lives. We have been told, in this kind of context, not to think and allow ourselves to get into the grip of a jargon, but to just look. Well, what is it that shows that, to take Wittgenstein's example, belief in the Last Judgment has obviously nothing in common with a hypothesis?

D.Z.P.: I think that if we do look at the role this belief plays in at least many believers' lives, we find that it is not a hypothesis, a conjecture, that some dreadful event is going to happen so many thousand years hence. We see this by recognizing that a certain range of reactions is ruled out for the believer. What I mean is this: if it were a conjecture about a future event, he might say, 'I believe it is going to happen' or 'Possibly it might happen' or 'I'm not sure; it may happen', and so on. But that range of reactions plays no part in the believer's belief in the Last Judgment. It is not a conjecture about the future, but, as it were, the framework, the religious framework, within which he meets fortune, misfortune, and the evil that he finds in his own life and in life about him.

J.R.J.: It would seem, then, that you could say that a genuine religious belief has a certain firmness which is quite peculiar to itself. That indeed, in a sense, the expression of a genuine religious belief could be described as the firmest of all judgments. Well, I wonder what is the character of this firmness, because it doesn't seem to mean the same thing as, for example, firmly grounded; because, of course, the whole notion of grounding, of obtaining good evidence, of weighing evidence, is right out of place here. What, then, is the character of the firmness?

D.Z.P.: Well, certainly the firmness does not mean, as you say, what it means in 'firmly grounded prediction'. Wittgenstein considers the example of a man who said, 'I had a dream last night in which I dreamt of the Last Judgment, and now I know what it is.' Well,

Wittgenstein says, if you compare that with a prediction of what weather we are going to get next week, it isn't any kind of prediction. 'I had a dream – therefore – Last Judgment.' We don't know what to make of that, if it is taken as an inference. So, in that sense, one might say the belief in the Last Judgment isn't firm at all, isn't well-established at all. So what could be meant, then, by firm belief here? Wittgenstein suggested that belief in religion has much more this role: I have this picture of the Last Judgment before my mind whenever, perhaps, I am tempted to perform a despicable deed. It regulates my thinking. It is firm in that it is to this picture that I appeal in such situations as these.

J.R.J.: If this, then, is the sort of firmness that a religious belief has, that is to say, not at all the firmness of a well-founded hypothesis or conjecture, what, then, is the non-believer doing when he rejects belief? You see, in not having a use for what you have called 'the picture', and in rejecting it because it has no force or significance in his life at all, is he then, or could he then be said to be, contradicting the believer?

D.Z.P.: In his lectures, Wittgenstein suggests that in certain cases, anyway, the non-believer would not be contradicting the believer. He takes the example of a man who, when he is ill, says, 'This is a punishment from God.' Wittgenstein asks, 'What am I saying if I say that this plays no part in my life? Am I contradicting the man who does believe this?'[3] Wittgenstein wants to deny this. What he would say is: 'It plays no part in my life at all; this collection of words means nothing to me, in the sense that it does not regulate my life; I do not adhere to it; I do not aspire to what it stands for.

Therefore, I am not involved in the same form of life as the man who does regulate his life by this picture and aspires to it.' On the other hand, if I said, 'There is a German aeroplane overhead'⁴ and you doubted this, we would both be participating in the same activity, namely, locating the German aeroplane; we would be appealing to the same criteria: I would be certain, you would be doubtful. But if I say that the idea of a Last Judgment plays no part in my life, then I am saying that in this respect you are on an entirely different plane from me; we are not participating in the same language-game, to use Wittgenstein's phrase, at all.

J.R.J.: It looks, then, that no evidence could count against or for; in that no evidence can count for, then, of course, it follows that no evidence can count against, what might naïvely be called the truth of these pictures. And yet, we know well, from experience and from the history of religions, that belief, religious belief, is something which can be undermined by scepticism; and scepticism would be in this case scepticism concerning what is thus naïvely called the truth of the picture. But, when this happens – and this is what interests me – when belief is thus undermined, or weakened, it then looks as though the picture itself begins to lose its hold on the life of the believer. And I wonder what this really signifies? Doesn't it suggest that there is some sort of internal relation between the weight or force of the picture – and I mean by that, it's having weight for me – and the state of my mind that is capable of being undermined by doubt? This seems to reintroduce the notion of a literal truth, as against a literal falsity, you see. It is in this kind of connection that doubt and scepticism work upon people's minds, and it looks as though it does do its job here. When there is this corrosion by doubt, the pictures are somehow corroded; they lose their hold.

D.Z.P.: I think this is an extremely important and difficult region to be reflecting about, and the best I can do, I think, is to make the following initial distinction. Let us distinguish between, on the one hand, someone, that is, a given believer, for whom the force of the Last Judgment no longer means anything. In his life, this picture of the Last Judgment means nothing at all, whereas it used to once. Now, what has happened here, I suggest, is that the *attention* of the individual has been won over either by a rival secular picture, or, of course, by wordliness, etc. Because his energies are now focused in another direction, this picture which was once powerful in his life, has lost its grip. Interestingly enough, when you say that the notion of literal truth is reintroduced, I suggest that it is reintroduced in this way: that when the old force of the picture is lost, the new force it has is that of a literal picture, which, as far as I can see, is simply a matter of superstition. But we might want to distinguish between the case of the picture losing its hold for a given individual, with religious pictures losing their hold anyway, not through the fault of any particular individual, but because of changes in the culture. Certain religious pictures decline, and yet you can't ask, 'But whose fault is it that they are declining?' You can't trace the decline to the biographical details of the life of any single individual.

J.R.J.: This cannot be done because it is a decay of belief which is affecting a whole culture or a whole epoch. Couldn't we be said to be living in such a period today – a period of what you might call prevalent disbelief? And I would be interested to know what you would say to this: why doesn't it make sense, then, in a period such as this, of the decay of belief, to suppose a group of people – of well-minded people – trying to bring about a renewal of faith, possibly from within a religious context or even from entirely without it; people with a secular background, noting the effect of the decay of belief on the morals of the culture generally, trying to bring about a renewal of faith by devising new and more acceptable pictures, and then trying to induce belief in them? Why is this somehow nonsensical? Why couldn't such a thing work?

D.Z.P.: I think this is linked to a point that we have neglected. So far, we have been concerned to emphasize that these religious beliefs are not conjectures, or hypotheses, with insufficient evidence for them. The beliefs are not empirical propositions. Once this is said, many philosophers assume that the beliefs must be human attitudes, values conferred, as it were, by individuals on to the world about them. But this does not follow and is in fact untrue. It is important to recognize that these pictures have a life of their own, a possibility of sustaining those who adhere to them. Part of the answer, though I think not the complete answer, to the question why it would be nonsensical to imagine theologians, let us say, creating pictures – new pictures – to meet the crisis of the age, the declining faith that they perceive about them, is that whatever they created would precisely be their creation, and you would have a curious reversal of the emphasis needed in religion, where the believer does not want to say that he measures these pictures and finds that they are all right or finds that they are wanting. On the contrary, the believers wish to claim that it isn't they who measure the pictures, since in a sense, the pictures measure them; they are the measure in terms of which they judge themselves. They do not judge the picture. Or again, to link with the earlier points we made, when people do judge the picture that is the time when they are beginning either to rebel against it, or when the picture is beginning to lose its hold on their lives as individuals.

J.R.J.: Yes, I agree with this, but there seems to me to be another thing that could be added to that. Isn't it, or wouldn't it be, precisely the element of believing as part of a tradition of belief that would be wanting or lacking in this attempt on the part of a group of people to bring about a renewal of faith by devising new pictures? You see, this group of would-be reformers wouldn't be dealing with a faith nourished by time and handed down from the past within which certain pictures are to be found. They would, rather, be presenting their new-fangled pictures first, and then trying to get people to believe them. Well, now, in such a situation, it seems to me, pictures degenerate into mere pictures; but – and this is interesting – not because they would be in the nature of hypotheses or conjectures for which the evidence is found wanting. Not that at all, but because they would be, as it were, trying to become, or trying to be made to become, operative as beliefs outside the sphere of, or you might say, in the absence of the surroundings of, belief – all that goes with believing in a tradition of belief, I mean, in an historical faith. I can't see that anything could be a substitute for that.

D.Z.P.: I agree entirely. This makes it necessary to say something about our use of the term 'picture'.

Sometimes, at a casual glance, it might look as if by 'pictures' we meant what you have now referred to as 'mere pictures'. Indeed, many philosophers of religion today have spoken of devising new pictures, finding new symbols, to communicate the essence of the divine to people. It's as if there were a deliberate *use* of the picture to communicate the essence of the divine. 'We now find that that picture isn't working, so let us revise what is called, naïvely, our image of God.' 'Our image of God must go', we are told. As if, independently of the picture, we have a notion of divinity. You then compare the picture with this notion and you say, 'Oh, well, it's not doing its job properly', and we have another picture. Wittgenstein stressed in his lectures that the whole weight may be in the picture. The picture is not a picturesque way of saying something else. It says what it says, and when the picture dies, something dies with it, and there can be no substitute for that which dies with the picture.

J.R.J.: Well, could this, then, have the implications that when the picture, which is a picture of the divine, as it were, which is God, having a role through faith in the whole life of a believer, is corroded by doubts and scepticism, the picture can be said to have died; but that when the picture dies or decays or is phased out in a whole culture, that in a sense, on your own presuppositions, God could be said to have died?

D.Z.P.: Yes, this is a difficulty that some people have felt about this way of talking. For instance, if you said that certain modes of moral conduct were to pass away, some people might say that there would be no goodness in the world any more. So why do we not want to say that if these pictures were to die, God dies, as it were, with the pictures? I think the answer to that, though I don't see this very clearly, is that the desire to say that God dies is literal-mindedness attempting to reassert itself. The point is that from within the picture something can be said now about such a time, that is, a time when people might turn their backs on it altogether. What can be said is that in such a time, people will have turned their backs on God. In other words, if people believe, there is nothing within belief which allows them to say that God can die. What they say is that there may come a time when people will turn their backs on God.

J.R.J.: It is as though you were saying that although the picture has, in one sense, died, not only in the lives of particular individuals, but even prevalently through the whole of a culture, it is still possible to speak from within the picture.

D.Z.P.: I am saying that it is possible for believers to say something now about such a time. You may find, of course – perhaps we do find – that only a handful of people do derive sustenance from this picture. But a picture may die in a culture because believing in it is not an isolated activity. To call the belief a language-game can be misleading if it does suggest an isolated activity. Other cultural changes can affect people's worship. For example, in *Brave New World* there is a decline in the notion of moral responsibility. In such a society one can see, without too much difficulty, how the notion of God as a Judge might also be in decline.

J.R.J.: So that, in that kind of society, the picture 'Last Judgment' would have no power over people's lives. But the interesting thing is that it wouldn't be this because it was a hypothesis for which people found that there wasn't sufficient evidence. It is not as a weak hypothesis that it declines, but because everything else surrounding it has declined out of that particular society.

D.Z.P.: As I said at the outset, we aimed to do no more in this discussion than to point out a direction in which the hold of a certain jargon could be avoided, a jargon which forces us to think of religious beliefs either as hypotheses about some future events or as human attitudes in which values are conferred on the world by the believers. In trying to elucidate what such a direction involves we have discussed what kind of beliefs religious beliefs are; the kind of firmness they have; in what sense they are unshakeable for the believer; on the other hand, what can happen to a believer when an unshakeable belief begins to lose its hold on him, and he becomes an unbeliever – what happens to him then; and also what is happening despite all his efforts to believe; what is happening in the culture in which he does believe, where, as it were, the surroundings from which the religious picture is nourished are changing, so bringing about changes in the nature of that religious picture itself.

References

1. This discussion first took place on B.B.C. Radio.
2. Wittgenstein, Ludwig, *Lectures and Conversations on Aesthetics,*

Belief and Loss of Belief

Psychology and Religious Belief, ed. Barrett, Cyril, Blackwell, 1966. The lectures on religious belief belong to a course of lectures on belief given by Wittgenstein some time during the summer of 1938.

3. These are not quotations.

4. Wittgenstein's example.

VII Religion and Epistemology: some Contemporary Confusions

There can be little doubt that contemporary philosophy of religion has benefited little from Wittgenstein's later epistemology. This is evident particularly in discussions of whether knowledge of God is possible. Religious and epistemological questions are frequently confused with each other to the detriment of both. In this chapter I shall consider three philosophers whose work illustrates the kind of confusion to which I wish to draw attention.

The problem with which the philosophers I have in mind have concerned themselves is not the problem of whether a *particular* claim to have had an experience of God is genuine or not, but rather the problem of whether *any* such claim is genuine. Doubts about the authenticity of religious claims are common enough. The Bible is full of them. Saying that something is of God does not make it so. Testimonies are not self-authenticating. Members of the Church are well aware of this fact. Spirits, however impressive, must be discerned to see whether they are of God. In order to do so, reference is made to the doctrines of the Church, and to the role which the 'religious experience' plays in the life of the person concerned. Such criteria for distinguishing between the genuine and the false are found, of course, *within* religion. Despite diversity and disagreement, one does have broad grounds which determine what could and what could not be of God.[1] But when contemporary philosophers of religion have asked whether knowledge of God is possible, they have sought for a justification of these grounds and criteria. A request is being made to show that the criteria which determine what is and what is not of God are *themselves* of God! If this is a religious question, one set of criteria is being challenged by another, and the philosophical request for a justification is merely redirected to the new criteria. My difficulty is in finding any meaning in this philosophical request for a *general* justification. I have yet to see an intelligible account of it. It reminds one of Toulmin's report of a remark by Wittgenstein 'that those philosophers who asked for a "justification" of science were like the Ancients, who felt there must be an Atlas to support the Earth on his shoulders (Cambridge University Moral Science Club: 14 November 1946).'[2] The requests for a 'foundation' for religion as such are but another example of seeking justifications beyond the stage where it makes sense to do so.

The first philosopher I want to discuss, Professor John Hick, says that anyone who reaches the above conclusion defends what he calls *the autonomy of religious language*.[3] I am not sure what Hick means by this phrase. If it is meant to imply that religion does not have significance for the whole of a person's life, it is not a thesis that I or some others whom Hick has in mind would care to defend. Hick says that the view he wants to attack 'draws its inspiration philosophically from the later teachings of Wittgenstein'.[4] Taking him at his word, I shall confine myself to a discussion of some of the theses which Hick thinks this view entails:

> One effect of this position is to make religious utterances immune to philosophical criticism. It is now not appropriate to ask for *grounds* of religious belief. Neither is it appropriate to ask for the *meaning* of 'God exists' if the request implies that there might be some other answer than a spelling out in religious terms of the respects in which God is real.[5]

I wonder what sort of account of the reality of God could be given which was not religious? It would be interesting to hear it; just as interesting as it would be to hear a non-musical account of the reality of music or a non-scientific account of the reality of science. In fairness to Hick, he says that the view he is attacking is importantly right in stressing that religious faith is not the product of philosophical reasoning. This being so, it is difficult to assess the force of his earlier criticisms. The criticisms are made in the name of 'the Christian believer', and they are made in forceful terms: 'The unacceptable feature of the position is that by treating religious language as autonomous—as a language-game with its own rules, or a speech activity having meaning only within its own borders—it deprives religious statements of "ontological" or "metaphysical" significance.'[6]

Were it not for the fact that Hick goes on to give a number of examples, I should have no idea of what he meant by ontological or metaphysical significance. But having examined his examples, I fail to see why they should have been given this description. Hick tells us that the ordinary believer has always supposed that 'God loves mankind' refers to an ultimate order of facts. God exists whether anyone believes in Him or not. God is a personal Mind who enters into relationships with other people. These relationships, and the character of God, are open to certain objections. For example, in so far as they are said to show love, evil counts against them. Hick's conclusion is that religious truth, like most other kinds of truth, must be measured by its conformity with or deviation from certain facts.

How does the so-called autonomous position reject all this? It is supposed to do so by confining 'religious truth-claims within the enclosed realm of the religious speech activity itself'.[7] Apparently, the conclusion which follows from this is that 'The logical implications of religious statements do not extend across the borders of the *Sprachspiel* into assertions concerning the character of the universe beyond the fragment of it which is the religious speech of human beings'.[8]

There are many confusions involved in these arguments. First, Hick confuses *conditions* of intelligibility with the *content* of what is said. It is true that religious concepts have their meaning within a certain form of life, but this does not imply that these concepts *say* anything about a form of life. The institution of religion is the condition of the possibility of meaning for concepts such as 'eternity', 'divine forgiveness', 'sin', 'grace', etc., but the meaning of these concepts, what they say, has nothing to do with institutions. This is an elementary point, but, unless I am mistaken, Hick is guilty of this confusion. Religious beliefs may tell one something about everything, but one must pay attention to the grammar of religious language to discover what that something is. Religion is not everything in the universe, but it does not follow that for *that* reason religion does not say anything about the world *as a whole*.

Second, despite all Hick's protests against the Wittgensteinian thesis that religion has within itself its own criteria of intelligibility, we find him, in his attempt to refute it, appealing to what he takes to be the actual beliefs of religious people – that is, to an alleged religious usage. To what else could one appeal? The position, then, whether Hick likes it or not, is that he and 'the autonomist' both appeal to religious language. On the other hand, Hick is quite right in thinking that there are important differences between the account he gives of religious belief and the account which, say, Norman Malcolm has given of religious belief.[9] How is one to choose between them? There is no appeal beyond the content of the respective portrayals; one has to judge whether the given account does justice to the complex network of behaviour which the 'religious belief' may refer to. One has a vast and various range of persons, all claiming to be religious believers. I do not deny, then, that there are people whose conception of God is similar to that outlined by Hick. There are some people the truth of whose religion depends on the way things go in their lives. Things may not go well here and now, but unless the ultimate facts, the eschatological situation, are favourable in some sense or other, faith has been a hoax and a failure. For Hick, the kind of difference religion makes to life is the difference between a set of empirical facts being or not being the case. This belief is illustrated by a comment I heard a mother make about her mentally handicapped child: 'Only my religious faith keeps me going. Of one thing I am sure:

my child's place in heaven is secure.' It is difficult, without having an opportunity to question further, to be sure of what such a hope amounts to. On Hick's account, the mother would be saying, 'It is terrible for my child at the moment, but he is to be compensated later on.' Her hope is in certain facts being realized.

Although I sympathize with the mother's hope, I do not find it impressive religiously. Indeed, I should want to go further and say that it has little to do with religion, being much closer to superstition. Two other mothers of mentally handicapped children expressed what their religious faith meant to them in very different terms. One of them discussed the view that there is a *prima facie* incompatibility between belief in God and the terrible-ness of having a mentally handicapped child. People kept asking her why such a thing should have happened to her, to which she replied, 'Why shouldn't it have happened to me?' I found this answer extremely impressive, although I suspect that it needs a respect for a certain kind of religious belief to find it so. The second mother had been a teacher before becoming a mother. She had been aware of the problem of handicapped children, but closed her mind to it. It was more con-venient to teach normal children. She prayed to God for a son. When he was born she said that God had answered her prayer. She then discovered that her son was mentally handicapped. This forced her to re-think her whole attitude towards prayer and towards children. She did not suggest that God had sent the child to her *in order* to change her attitude or as a rebuke for her former one. Such thoughts were foreign to her. What she did say was that she had come closer to God through the birth of her son. She said that for the first time she knew what it meant to cast her burden upon the Lord.

Both mothers refuse to look upon belief in God as an explanatory hypothesis. They both, in what they say, participate in the love of God, a love which will not let them go, whatever the circumstances.[10] Their attitudes remind one of Simone Weil's profound remark: 'The extreme greatness of Christianity lies in the fact that it does not seek a supernatural remedy for suffering, but a supernatural use for it.'[11] Hick's eschatological propaganda is a search for remedies, a requisite for compensation, and as such seems foreign to deep religious faith.

I am not primarily concerned in this chapter with the difficult question of religious attitudes towards evil. I mentioned the above examples to show that Hick's paradigm of the religious believer can certainly be questioned, and would be rejected by many. I do not wish to defend those people whose religious beliefs can be described adequately in Hick's terms. I only wish to stress that there is another kind of belief in God. The difference between them could be brought out by comparing the roles which worship plays in the lives of the respective believers. But in any case, one must examine *what is said*. Hick has failed to show what is wrong with this philosophical procedure.

The second philosopher I want to discuss, Professor Ronald Hepburn, also feels that it is inadequate to appeal to religious language to discover what religion means. His main objection is that to do so would be to identify God with His manifestations in the world. It is difficult to see how this conclusion is arrived at, since if one *does* appeal to what religious believers say, one finds that very many of them say that the world depends on

God. Hepburn says: 'Within traditional Christian
theology, . . . questions about the divine existence cannot be deflected into the question, "Does 'God' play an
intelligible role in the language-game?"'[12]

But why should anyone suppose that a Wittgensteinian thesis about meaning involves this conclusion? All it
states is that the meaning of God's reality is to be found
in His divinity, which is expressed in the role worship
plays in people's lives. This does not imply that God's
reality, divinity, or worship, can be equated with
language-games; that is not what they *mean*! Like Hick,
Hepburn is guilty of confusing a linguistic context with
what is said.

To some extent Hepburn anticipates this criticism,
and in an attempt to meet it he says that if one does
appeal to religious language, one will find that God is
thought of as *really* transcendent. Hepburn, like Hick,
ends up by appealing to actual religious usage of language in order to find out what it means to believe in
God. Such a reference is not surprising, but one wonders
in the light of it what becomes of the opening attack
against Wittgensteinianism in philosophy of religion.
One must consider Hepburn's account of what religious
believers are saying on its merits. As in Hick's case, the
account seems nearer superstition than religion. Hepburn is convinced that God is thought of as an *individual*. We are not told how much this involves. The
believer, Hepburn claims, experiences God as an
intrusion in his life, but no analysis of this experience is
given. In Hepburn's terminology it would not be far
removed from an intrusion by a visitor from outer
space! Hepburn and Hick are obsessed by God's *real*
existence, and, for them, this seems to mean existing as

human beings do, or perhaps as the moon and the stars exist. Positivism and empiricism have had an obvious influence on their thinking. There is no attempt by them to discuss the difference between believing in a God who may or may not exist, and believing in an eternal God. It is no exaggeration to say that the very possibility of understanding what religion is about depends on this distinction being drawn. Hick says of the existence of God:

> I do not know how it could ever be demonstratively proved that Amos and Paul and the other biblical writers presupposed the real existence of the God whom they worshipped; but I also think that anyone who doubts that this presupposition operated in their minds must be blinded in a very sophisticated way to the natural and ordinary meanings of words.[13]

I am suggesting, on the contrary, that it is Hick and Hepburn who are blinded, though not in a sophisticated way, to the depth grammar of religious discourse. They are too impressed by the surface grammar of religious language, which is the source of the conceptual confusion in this context. For example, has Hick ever asked himself *how* Paul could say that he worshipped *the same* God as Amos? Surely not in the same way in which two astronomers decide whether they are talking about the same star![14] What does Hick mean by the *real* existence of God, and what does Hepburn mean by calling God an *entity* or an *individual*? Would either of them want to say that God has a biography? It seems clear to me that there is no question of *finding out*, where the reality of God is concerned. Despite the protests of these philosophers against an appeal to religious language to find out what is meant by the reality of God, what they have done is to impose the grammar of *another* mode of discourse on religion – namely, our talk about physical objects. Thus, Hick merely begs the whole question by talking about 'the natural and ordinary meaning of words'.

Once philosophers begin to ignore religious criteria of meaningfulness, epistemological scepticism about religion is inevitable. If all that is said about God is a mere approximation, mere hints or signs of divinity, an unbridgeable logical gap is opened up between religious experience, worship, and religious discourse on the one hand, and the reality of God on the other. The problem then, as Hepburn says, is how one moves from the world to God. On this view, one can no longer equate worship with knowledge of God. Worship may not be what it claims to be. The believer may say that he believes that the world is God's creation, and that humanity has fallen from grace and stands in need of redemption. But Hepburn replies, 'Again, we are only speaking of observable phenomena, and of how we interpret, what we "make of" those phenomena.'[15] Hepburn finds himself in this dilemma because he fails to see that religious concepts are not *interpretations* of phenomena. Philosophers speak as if one had some constant factors called 'the phenomena', of which religion and humanism are competing interpretations. But what are these phenomena? Religious language is not an interpretation of how things are, but determines how things are for the believer. The saint and the atheist do not interpret the same world in different ways. They see different worlds.

The epistemological scepticism, latent, at least, in the

views of Hick and Hepburn, becomes explicit in the views of the third philosopher I wish to discuss – namely, Professor I. T. Ramsey. Ramsey's scepticism is particularly evident in his Whidden Lectures, delivered at McMaster University in 1963, and published under the title *Models and Mystery*.[16]

Ramsey confuses epistemological and religious questions. He recognizes, quite rightly, that the concept of mystery has an important place in religious belief. No one would deny that. But, of course, to understand *this* concept of mystery one must elucidate what it means to believe in God, what it means to see all things in His hands. This is not what Ramsey does. He equates the concept of reality found in religion with the *general question* about the nature of reality in which metaphysicians and epistemologists are interested. In metaphysics and epistemology, one raises the 'big' philosophical question of how knowledge is possible *at all*; one conducts an enquiry into the conditions of the possibility of discourse. Language, whatever its particular manifestations, must exhibit distinctions between following and not following conceptual rules; it must show that it makes a difference whether one says one thing rather than another. What following a conceptual rule amounts to, what kind of difference saying something makes, can only be elucidated by clarifying the grammar of the discourse in question. Ultimately, one would have to appeal to the criteria of intelligibility operative in the given mode of discourse. Wittgenstein stressed that each mode of discourse is not part of some all-embracing reality; it is what it is.

Evidently, Ramsey, Hick, and Hepburn feel that this will not do. Is not God thereby being confined to the mode of discourse in which talking to Him and about Him is meaningful? This misgiving is a complete misunderstanding. It rests on a confusion of logical and religious priorities. To say that religion does not explain every form of human activity is not to restrict or reject any religious claim. It is simply to reject the view that religion stands in an *explanatory* relation to all other social phenomena. Belief in God is certainly a belief about everything, but that does not mean that it is another way of saying everything there is to say. This is what Ramsey cannot recognize. The game is given away at the outset when he tells us:

> . . . my thesis will be that our various disciplines, despite their necessary and characteristic differences, nevertheless have a common feature of great significance, a feature which is often overlooked and frequently misunderstood: the use they make of models. It is by the use of models that each discipline provides its understanding of a mystery which confronts them all.[17]

It is impossible to give an intelligible account of what 'the same mystery' means in this context, since any distinction between sameness and difference will be a distinction found in a particular mode of discourse. Ramsey is wedded to a Lockean theory of knowledge. Just as Locke held that ideas come to a subject from a world which is never directly perceived, so Ramsey holds that a mysterious universe prompts disclosures of itself in the subject. The views of Hick and Hepburn lead to scepticism about the possibility of religious knowledge. Ramsey's arguments open the door to scepticism about any kind of knowledge. Starting with

religious mystery, he ends up with a mysterious epistemology! By confusing religious and logical priorities,
Ramsey thinks that religious mystery is the key to *all*
forms of discourse. The consequences of such a view are
disastrous. Let us consider two examples.

First, Ramsey argues that the natural sciences are
rooted in mystery. He speaks of the theory of the linear
propagation of light as rooted in disclosure, a disclosure
generated by the edge of a shaft of sunlight coming
through a window into a room, and a mathematical
straight line. Ramsey's thesis is that no third-person
assertion of the behaviour of natural phenomena can
ever be complete, because there is a 'subjectivity which
is logically demanded by the objectivity of all the
behaviourist's data'.[18] In other words, any model one
adopts to explain behaviour, because it will be expressed
in terms of third-person assertions, remains logically
incomplete, since implicit in the model is a reference to
the subject for whom the model is a disclosure of a
universe which is abidingly mysterious. Ramsey's agent
is a lonely figure, to whom, via models, disclosures
come of the universe outside him. But without reference
to *the context* in which such disclosures occur, no sense
can be made of such occurrences. Once a specific context *is* introduced, the disclosure, the insight, call it
what you will, cannot play the fundamental role which
Ramsey wants to attribute to it.

Moments of inspiration may account for the origin
of new scientific procedures, but this does not mean that
they are disclosures of what is ultimately mysterious. On
the contrary, Stephen Toulmin has pointed out how
theoretical models can grow out of regularities in
natural phenomena with which the untrained man is

perfectly familiar.[19] Furthermore, the adoption of a model depends on its successful use, on what it enables one to explain. What one wants to explain will be determined to a large extent by the course of the science in question up to that point. So the decision to adopt the model cannot be fundamental in this context, since whether a model is adopted or not is not determined by anyone's decision to adopt it, but by whether it furthers the investigations in hand. Peter Winch makes this point very clearly.[20] He shows the importance of keeping two relations in mind: (*a*) the relation between the scientist and the phenomena he is observing, and (*b*) the relation between the scientist and his fellow scientists. Winch says that 'writers on scientific "methodology" too often concentrate on the first and overlook the importance of the second'.[21] This is true of Ramsey. His agent is simply confronted by phenomena, which disclose themselves in various ways. But, as Winch points out, although the 'phenomena being investigated present themselves to the scientist as an *object* of study', and he observes them and notices certain facts about them, 'to say of a man that he does this presupposes that he already has a mode of communication in the use of which rules are already being observed',[22] and this brings one back to the relation between the scientist and his fellow scientists. Earlier, Winch gives an example to illustrate the point:

> For instance, someone with no understanding of the problems and procedures of nuclear physics would gain nothing from being present at an experiment like the Cockcroft-Walton bombardment of lithium by hydrogen; indeed, even the description of what he

saw in those terms would be unintelligible to him, since the term 'bombardment' does not carry the sense in the context of the nuclear physicist's activities that it carries elsewhere. To understand what was going on in this experiment he would have to learn the nature of what nuclear physicists do; and this would include learning the criteria according to which they made judgments of identity.[23]

It is clear, then, that the insight of the agent cannot be fundamental in explaining the nature of scientific activity. Neither can disclosures with a one-to-one observer-phenomena relation play such a role. What Winch has shown is that insights and disclosures must be tested to see whether they be of science. Ramsey's thesis falsifies the facts by reversing them. Science does not 'depend' on disclosures or insights, since it is scientific criteria that determine what is and what is not to count as a disclosure or an insight. These criteria are *within* science. By confusing religion and epistemology, Ramsey thinks that, since religion, in a certain sense, is about everything, and since mystery is important in religion, everything must be rooted in mystery. Science itself becomes a range of various models which hints at the mysterious universe which confronts it. Thus Ramsey introduces ignorance and scepticism into science where they need not prevail.

As our second example of Ramsey's epistemological confusion, let us consider characteristically human behaviour. Here, the confusion thickens. Ramsey pays lip-service to the central point Winch wishes to emphasize – namely, that there is an essential difference between the natural scientist's observation of natural phenomena, and the social scientist's observation of social behaviour. In the former case, the identification of relevant and irrelevant characteristics is determined by the rules of the method of observation, but in the latter case, by the rules operative in that which is observed – namely, human activity. When Winch criticizes Popper's statement that social institutions are just explanatory models introduced by social scientists for their own purposes, Ramsey seems to agree. Winch had said:

> The idea of war, for instance, which is one of Popper's examples, was not invented by people who wanted to *explain* what happens when societies come into armed conflict. . . . The concept of war belongs essentially to my behaviour (if my country is at war). But the concept of gravity does not belong essentially to the behaviour of a falling apple in the same way: it belongs rather to the physicist's *explanation* of the apple's behaviour.[24]

Ramsey seems to endorse the view that 'Popper allows for no genuine social community, no genuine social relations, no distinctive social interaction between men'.[25] But almost immediately he shows that he has missed Winch's point by going on to say: 'Supposing then – so far with Winch – that we readily acknowledge the need in social studies not only for models with a scientific status but for distinctively personal models – models of persons in relation.'[26]

But the whole point of Winch's argument was to show that forms of life, or persons in relation (to use an unhappy phrase), are *not models at all*; they do not point beyond themselves to a mystery which they disclose, but have within themselves their criteria of intelligibility. Ramsey even calls 'friendship' a model![27] But, to parody Winch, friendship is not a model invented by people to explain what happens when there are certain bonds between people. The concept of friendship belongs essentially to my behaviour (if I have friends or know what it means to have friends).

It is clear that Ramsey's fundamental reason for rejecting the models of natural science as explanations of human behaviour has nothing to do with the important distinction drawn by Winch, but, rather, is based on his own special views on the difference between participating in and observing human behaviour. It is here, in the activity of 'I', that Ramsey claims to find the parallel to the concept of mystery found in religion. This is brought out by his criticisms of Richard C. Atkinson's paper, 'The Use of Models in Experimental Psychology'.[28] Ramsey argues that no adequate account of human action can be given in terms of stimulus and response, but his main reason for criticizing Atkinson is because he thinks he has blurred the distinction between participant and observer. For, Ramsey argues, 'to participate and to observe are rarely equivalent – to participate in a kiss for example is vastly different from merely observing one'.[29] But notice what has happened here: Ramsey has changed the argument completely by introducing an ambiguity into the notion of an observer. We have two kinds of observer: (*a*) The social scientist who is said to observe human behaviour in terms appropriate to the natural sciences. (*b*) The ordinary way in which one man can observe another man kissing a woman.

The criticism of (*a*) was that it involved equating 'action' with 'movement', and the 'subject' with an 'organism'. But that cannot be a criticism of (*b*). Yet Ramsey seems to take this to be the case. He says: 'To act is to participate; but what the observer observes, and all he observes, is movement.'[30] But in the case of (*b*) this is simply not true. If a person sees two people kissing, he does so by virtue of his grasp of the concept of kissing. The concept may not be the same within all traditions. Kissing may be a form of greeting, a way of showing affection, or it may be reserved for a ritualistic sign of betrothal. Observing a kiss, therefore, entails understanding *the act*, and is different in kind from observing movement. It is this difference in kind that Ramsey does not take due account of. For instance, consider his treatment of the following example: '. . . no one puts his arm around his girl-friend and speaks of their relation in terms of available response alternatives, or reinforcement parameters. It is true that the psychologist on the seat opposite may do all this; but my important point is that he on the seat opposite is not the man with his arm around the girl.'[31]

But Ramsey's point is not important at all. The reason why the psychologist's description is not an account, and logically could not be an account, of the action, is that it ignores the context in which and from which the act has its meaning. It has nothing to do with Ramsey's murky metaphysics about the participant-observer distinction. It is not because the psychologist is not the man with his arm around the girl that he fails to give an account of the action. Another observer who says, 'He has his arm around his girl-friend,' does so quite successfully. This will not do for Ramsey: 'The ideal of logical completion is never a third-person assertion; it is a first-person assertion. *He does X* necessarily carries with it a pair of invisible quotation-marks, so that it is to be set in some such frame as "I am saying . . .", and without this wider frame the third-person assertion is logically incomplete.'[32]

Ramsey's problem of 'logical incompleteness' is an unnecessary one. To grasp what is involved in a social act involves two conditions. Consider these conditions in the case of the act of kissing. First, in order for *A* to kiss *B* he must live in a society in which there is a concept of kissing. If he lives in a society in which there is no such concept, then, no matter how much *A*'s action may resemble kissing, he cannot be said to kiss *B*. Second, *A* himself must grasp the concept of kissing. For example, given that kissing is a ritualistic sign of betrothal, *A* must grasp the relation between the act of kissing and the fact of his betrothal with all that it implies. The grasping of the concept of kissing involves an understanding of what it means to say, 'He is kissing,' *and* of what it means to say, 'I am kissing.' But there is no mystery involved in the situation. It is simply not true to say that an account of kissing in terms of third-person assertions is logically incomplete, disclosing something to the agent about a mysterious universe. *Of course* there is a difference between saying, 'He is kissing,' and kissing oneself, but this difference is not explained by reference to anything other than the contexts in which kissing has its meaning. One does not have to refer to anything other than traditions of courtship to elucidate the difference between 'He has his arm around his girl-friend' and 'I have my arm around his girl-friend'! Once again we see how Ramsey's insistence on importing mystery into epistemology introduces ignorance where knowledge is attainable.

It remains to be shown that Ramsey is not even correct where the concept of *religious* mystery is concerned. It is not, as he thinks, associated with ignorance, nor does it necessitate 'mysterious epistemologies'. There is no contradiction in saying that one understands the concept of religious mystery. This is because religious mysteries are not like detective mysteries. If you understand a mystery that troubles detectives, then, for you, there is no mystery. In the case of detective mysteries one has a distinction between what as a matter of fact is unknown, and what can be known. Ignorance is of the essence of detective mysteries. But religious mysteries have no relation to ignorance. They do not refer to that which may be, but which as a matter of fact is not, known, but to what is logically unknowable. To understand what is meant by religious mystery is to understand how to *use* the concept of mystery – for example, in worship and meditation. Religious mystery is connected with what the saints have called 'the way of unknowing', with the folly of thinking that there are reasons for why things are as they are, and with the prohibition against idolatry: that is, against likening God to anything natural. Contrast this with Ramsey's elaborate epistemology, where, significantly, the concept of mystery is associated with ignorance. Ramsey's treatment of the concept provides no insight into the meaning of religion, since it ignores the role the concept of mystery plays there. As we have seen, as a result of his arguments, religious mysteries become epistemological mysteries. The latter are in fact self-contradictions, since the very life of epistemology depends on showing how knowledge is possible. Epistemologically, there must be criteria, formal or informal as the case may be, for the use of the concept of mystery. These *criteria* are not mysterious, and it is an elementary confusion to think that because this is so one has detracted something from the religious sense of mystery.

It seems to me that the religious concepts discussed by Professors Hick, Hepburn, and Ramsey have been abstracted from the human phenomena that lie behind them, and so have lost or changed their meaning. Philosophically, this is a direct result of their opposition to the lessons taught in Wittgenstein's later epistemology. Hick and Hepburn, as we saw, imposed an alien grammar on religious discourse, while Ramsey changed the religious concept of mystery into an epistemological theory. The shortcomings of their own epistemologies are exposed, it seems to me, in the following comment by Peter Winch:

> We cannot say . . . that the problems of philosophy arise out of language *rather than* out of the world, because in discussing language philosophically we are in fact discussing *what counts as belonging to the world*. Our idea of what belongs to the realm of reality is given for us in the language that we use. The concepts we have settle for us the form of experience we have of the world. (It may be worth reminding ourselves of the truism that when we speak of the world we are speaking of what we in fact mean by the expression 'the world': there is no way of getting outside the concepts in terms of which we think of the world. . . . The world *is* for us what is presented through those concepts. That is not to say that our concepts may not change; but when they do, that means that our concept of the world has changed too.) [33]

References

1. I have tried to show how essential it is to recognize such grounds if one is to be able to talk of religious experience at all in *The Concept of Prayer* (Routledge & Kegan Paul). See, especially, ch. 7, 'God's Voice and the Concept of Community'.
2. *The Place of Reason in Ethics*, C.U.P. Paperback Ed. 206n.
3. See 'Sceptics and Believers' in *Faith and the Philosophers*, ed. Hick, J.
4. *Ibid.*, 237.
5. *Ibid.*, 238.
6. *Ibid.*, 239.
7. *Ibid.*
8. *Ibid.*
9. See 'Anselm's Ontological Arguments', *Philosophical Review*, January 1960, and 'Is It a Religious Belief that "God Exists"?' in *Faith and the Philosophers*.
10. For a brilliant analysis of this religious concept of love see Kierkegaard's *Works of Love*, especially Part Two.
11. Simone Weil, *Waiting on God*, Fontana Ed., 73.
12. 'From World to God', *Mind*, January 1963, 41.
13. *Op. cit.*, 241.
14. I discussed this question at greater length in ch. 1, 'Philosophy, Theology, and the Reality of God'. See pp. 1–12.
15. *Op. cit.*, 40.
16. O.U.P., 1964.
17. *Op cit.*, 1.
18. *Ibid.*, 27.
19. *The Philosophy of Science*, H.U.L., 1953. See ch. 2.
20. See *The Idea of a Social Science*, 83.
21. *Ibid.*, 84–5.
22. *Ibid.*, 85.
23. *Ibid.*, 84.
24. *Ibid.*, 127.
25. *Op. cit.*, 37.
26. *Ibid.*
27. *Ibid.*, 40.
28. Published in *The Concept and the Role of the Model in Mathematics and Natural and Social Sciences*, ed. Kazemier, B. H., and Vuysje, D., Holland; D. Reidel, 1961.

29. *Op. cit.*, 25.
30. *Ibid.*
31. *Ibid.*, 28.
32. *Ibid.*, 27.
33. *Op. cit.*, 15.

VIII Philosophy and Religious Education[1]

> Here one still believes it is all a matter of Jesuits or Masons, witches or goblins, luck or exorcism, the *revolutionary hydra* or the *black wave of reaction*, the miracles of ignorance or those of science. Things are either windmills or they are giants; we comprehend no middle terms.

These words were spoken in frustration by Miguel de Unamuno when he saw the reaction to his philosophical work in Spain. Again and again when people considered his views, they insisted on forcing them into competing categories. For them, the important question was whether his views were those of a Catholic or a Protestant, a believer or a non-believer, a scholastic or a positivist. The philosophical problems Unamuno wrestled with were by-passed. Their relevance was determined by whether or not they served the interests of a particular cause: things were either windmills or giants. In this context, Unamuno had to battle alone, almost despairing because of the false choice people confronted him with, and because of the lack of middle terms. What did he have in mind when he spoke of this lack? Unamuno wanted to contrast the vision in which everything is seen in terms of a struggle for supremacy, where everything must either be a windmill or a giant, with the neutrality of philosophy. When he accused his contemporaries in Spain of failing to comprehend any middle terms, he was referring directly to their failure to understand the nature of such philosophical enquiry. Of course, no one would deny that Unamuno's philosophical reflections on religion did and do have an influence on people's religious beliefs and on people's opposition to religion. Be that as it may, this is a consequence rather than the point of Unamuno's philosophizing. The point of his enquiry was not to show that there is a God or that there is no God, but to ask what it means to say that there is a God or that there is no God.[2] These latter questions cut across the polemical confrontation between belief and unbelief. They are part of an activity of conceptual analysis, the aim of which is clarification not victory.

Why have I begun this paper by mentioning the troubles which Unamuno faced in Spain? I have done so because very similar troubles beset discussions concerning religious education in schools. Here too, I fear, things are either windmills or giants, with the protagonists comprehending no middle terms. More often than not, the discussion takes the form of a struggle, a battle for the minds of the young. The description of the battle depends on which side provides it. If we look in certain quarters, we find the battle described as the fight by enlightened and progressive parents, movements and authorities, to purge education from indoctrination and to rescue children from the grip of superstition. But if we look in other quarters, the description of the battle is very different. Here it is described as the attempt to defend basic values, and to show that the importance of religion permeates the whole of life. So under the respective banners battle commences. What is often lost sight of, however, is that the disagreement is supposed to be over a matter of education. Just as in the case of the content of Unamuno's philosophical investigations, the issue being discussed is made subordinate to the cause being supported. In the context of the discussion of religious education there is a great need to comprehend middle terms. Because of this, the neutrality of the philosophy of religion has much to offer to the discussion of this vexed question.

Unfortunately, however, the situation is more complex than I have indicated so far. I may well have given the impression that the situation which confronts us is one in which philosophers maintain an admirable neutrality, while religious and anti-religious factions carry out their militant propaganda concerning religion in schools. But that is certainly not the case. The present state of philosophy of religion, to a large extent, also betrays an ignorance of middle terms, and a desire to argue for or against religious beliefs, rather than to elucidate their nature. That being so, it is not surprising to find confusion resulting from the application of such philosophical conceptions to the question of religious education. By considering some aspects of this confusion and contrasting it with the philosophical neutrality I think desirable, I hope to shed a little light on the question of religion in schools.

Let us begin by attempting to summarize a fairly widespread attitude to teaching religion in schools, which is shared by philosophers who are sympathetic to religion and by philosophers who are antagonistic to religion. It amounts to something like this: at the very least there is no case at the moment for teaching religion in schools, since the truths which religions proclaim have, as yet, not been established. This attitude has been expressed by Professor Paul Hirst. He asks, 'What is the status of religious propositions? Is there here a domain of knowledge or simply one of beliefs?'[3] Hirst concludes that all we have is a domain of mere belief, and that therefore there is no justification for State-maintained schools to teach religion. He says that 'What knowledge we teach we teach because it comes up to publicly accepted rational tests, convinced that all those prepared to investigate the matter to the appropriate extent will agree on the results'.[4] But according to Hirst religious beliefs do not come up to the required standard: 'If in fact, as seems to be the case at present, there are no agreed public tests whereby true and false can be distinguished in religious claims, then we can hardly maintain that we have a domain of religious knowledge and truth.'[5] This being so, he argues, there is little justification for the inclusion of religion in an educational syllabus. Hirst does see glimmers of hope in the philosophical activities of the Neo-Thomists which, if realized, would show that religious beliefs have a rational foundation. His final conclusion, however, is not over-optimistic, since he describes his hopeful expectations as 'just crystal-gazing. In the present state of affairs, whatever other considerations might imply, philosophical considerations would seem to suggest that the 1944 legislation on religious education is unjustifiable.'[6] I shall argue that *philosophical* considerations alone lead to no such conclusion.

The view Hirst is advancing, one which is widespread among philosophers of religion, is that whereas religious beliefs may reflect the private experiences of individual believers, there is no way of knowing whether these experiences reflect what in fact is the case. Hirst asks:

> If I have an experience of encounter, how am I to know it is an experience of God and not an hallucination? If the core of the matter is simply commitment or decision, what is there in commitment that guarantees the truth of the beliefs? Private beliefs which lack rational justification may be true, but we cannot know that they are true without there being some public justification. And lacking that, we cannot lay claim to a domain of knowledge.[7]

But is the account Hirst gives of religious belief a recognizable one? Is it true that there are no public criteria in religion to distinguish between the true and the false, the deep and the shallow, or the genuine and the sham? Is it true that everything is a matter of personal decision, and that religious believers are never quite sure whether they are worshipping or suffering from hallucinations? No agreed public tests; think of the confusion which must reign in religious circles. In order to assess what Hirst is saying, we need, following Professor Bouwsma in a similar context, to

> imagine a linguistic cataclysm, something like what happened at the Tower of Babel. Perhaps you remember the Scripture, 'Come, let us go down, and then confuse their language that they may not understand one another's speech.' Presumably, in this case God took away their definitions, their rules, and their postulates, and the consequence was that the terms of their ordinary – or was it, then, extra-

ordinary? – language, were on that day in May
suddenly ambiguous and vague.[8]

Bouwsma was discussing the suggestion, made by Feigl
and Maxwell, that the terms of ordinary language are
notoriously ambiguous and vague. Professor Hirst
implies that a similar notoriety is true of religious language: no agreed public tests for truth and falsity. So
what Hirst asks us to imagine is not a general linguistic
cataclysm such as happened at the Tower of Babel, but
a limited linguistic cataclysm confined to religion. What
is involved in it? We can be helped to see this by listening to Bouwsma's account of the limited linguistic
cataclysm which took place with the Sears-Roebuck
mail-order catalogue. Before the event, people know
their way about the catalogue: 'People know what they
want, they have the money to buy what they want.
They study the catalogue, they make out the order,
send it off with cheque enclosed, and someone, Mr or
Mrs Sears, reads the order, puts the underwear in a box
and sends it to the Institute. It gets cold in Minnea-
polis.'[9] But suddenly all is changed:

> As for what the cataclysm did to the catalogue, what
> a time they had of it at Sears'. All the terms ambig-
> uous and vague! They couldn't fill an order right. A
> man seemed to want a rake and they gave him socks.
> It was all guess-work. People were returning articles
> they never wanted for others they never wanted. No
> one could say what he wanted and no one else could
> make out what it was he wasn't saying. It was
> exasperating. People made hands do what words
> wouldn't, and got their rakes. But in this case even
> money couldn't talk. Dollars made no sense. At one

o'clock Sears-Roebuck shut up shop, and, as at the Tower of Babel, Montgomery-Ward took over the business.[10]

A similar fate befell religious worshippers. Before the cataclysm, they knew what they were doing. They knew the difference between adoration and confession, petition and thanksgiving. But after the cataclysm chaos reigned: people thanked for their sins and asked for more, and their hymns greeted the morning at the end of the day. They asked for things they never wanted, but no one could say what he wanted, and no one else could say what it was he wasn't saying. Every time people called on God they never knew whether they were mistaken, or whether they were mistaken about their mistakes, or whether their mistaken views about their mistakes were mistakes. People read Tolstoy's story and seemed to understand Sergius's words when he concluded that Pashenka had served God while thinking that she was serving men, while he, thinking he was serving God, had in fact served men. But they only seemed to understand, since no one could be sure whether words meant to Sergius what they meant to him, or, indeed, whether words ever meant the same in religion to anyone. As at Sears', it was all guess-work.

So far we have been trying to see, with Professor Bouwsma's help, what sort of thing Professor Hirst might be asking us to envisage when he tells us that there are no agreed public tests whereby true and false can be distinguished in religious claims. But there is a further complication connected with this attempt. It is not at all certain that a reference to the limited linguistic cataclysm, even with all the difficulties involved in giving a coherent account of such an event, corresponds to what Hirst has in mind. In order to give some kind of account of the cataclysm, it was necessary to imagine a 'before' and an 'after'; to imagine what people were doing before the disaster befell them. Before their language became confused religious believers were able to worship, they knew how to use words like 'sinful', 'divine', 'church', etc., but after the cataclysm, as we have seen, they no longer knew their way about. But this is not what Hirst is saying. He is not saying that once upon a time there were agreed public tests for truth and falsity in religion which were lost in a linguistic cataclysm, but that there never have been such tests. In describing the effects of the cataclysm, we contrasted them with normality, but for Hirst what we described as cataclysmic is his description of normality! Hirst is not speculating about what might happen, but about what he claims is in fact the case.

What we have seen, however, is that what he claims about religion is not in fact true. There are various criteria recognized by religious believers for what can and what cannot be said to God and about God. It is not true that there are no tests for what is truly religious. Neither is it true that there are no tests for what is to count as religious as opposed to hallucinatory beliefs. Doctors do not look on church-going or worship as symptoms of religious mania. Furthermore, if a person says he has had a religious vision, it does not follow that he has had one. If a man said that God had told him in a vision to eliminate all coloured people from the face of the earth, this would not be accepted by the Christian community as a vision from God. So it is not all a matter of personal decision or commitment. Professor Hirst's fears about this are born of his failure to give any place to the notion of community in religion. It is little wonder that as a consequence he can find no starting-place to distinguish between what is of God and what is not.[11]

Professor Hirst is also worried by the fact that religious concepts do not come up to a required educational standard, by which he means that there is no guarantee that people will agree about them, no matter how long they discuss them. But if this is to be the test, much else besides religion would have to disappear from the school curriculum – for example, English literature and history. Professor Hirst suffers from a misplaced scepticism. He believes that in order that scepticism might be avoided, agreement must be sought in the sphere of discourse in question. But when historians disagree, they are disagreeing on historical questions. Certain interjections in the dispute would obviously be irrelevant. The fact that this is so shows that there is something being discussed here, and it would not make sense to be sceptical about that. There are disagreements about literary and historical questions – disagreements which, for all we know, may never be resolved. But the mere fact of such disagreement does not lead to general scepticism about history and literature. Unless the disputants had much in common, there would be no possibility of disagreement. Though there are important differences, a similar point can be made about moral disagreement. When people disagree on moral questions, it does not follow that anyone can say what he likes. On the contrary, not any viewpoint could be a moral viewpoint, and within differing viewpoints there are criteria for what can and cannot be said. Professor

Hirst seems to think that where there is no agreement in opinions, it is all a matter of personal decision. Clearly, this is not the case.

Professor Hirst might point out, with some justification, that there are important differences between religious beliefs and the examples I have mentioned hitherto. Unlike the previous examples, the dispute about religion which concerns the question of whether it ought to be taught in schools is not a dispute about a particular question within an accepted realm of discourse, but a dispute about a realm of discourse as such. So that a dispute between a believer and a non-believer over whether religion should be taught in schools is not like a dispute between two historians over a question in their subject. The historians are not disagreeing over whether history is true, whatever that might mean, whereas the truth of religious beliefs is precisely the issue at stake in the other disagreement. So although Hirst puts his point in a confused way when he says that 'What knowledge we teach we teach because it comes up to publicly accepted rational tests, convinced that all those prepared to investigate the matter to the appropriate extent will agree on the results',[12] he probably had in mind the question of the truth of religious beliefs as such, rather than disputed questions within an accepted mode of discourse. We have seen that there are criteria within religious traditions which distinguish between what can and cannot be said, what is true and what is false, what is deep and what is shallow, but this may cut no ice with Hirst. For him these criteria operate within a class of beliefs which are at best hypothetical. He may want to say that all the distinctions achieve is to distinguish between shrewd guesses and foolish ones, or between the more probable and the less probable. But there are difficulties in this point of view, since unless guesses were sometimes confirmed one could not have a distinction between shrewd and foolish guesses; unless probabilities were sometimes realized, one could not have a distinction between the more and the less probable. But Hirst wants to say that religious guesses or hypotheses are *never* confirmed. That is why we are so unsure of what we have on our hands here; that is why we cannot say whether we have in religion a domain of knowledge which can be taught. There is no escape from the context of conjecture, it seems. Professor Hirst concludes on these grounds that we do not have a domain of knowledge and truth where religious beliefs are concerned, but simply one of beliefs.

What we need here, however, is to compare what Hirst says about religious beliefs with their actual character. If we do this, we shall find, as we have done previously in this chapter, that his remarks are extremely misleading.

Clearly, when Hirst refers to religious *beliefs*, he has in mind a contrast with religious *knowledge*. For Hirst, beliefs are a second-best, things we should be cautious and not over-emphatic about. In making this distinction, he is, of course, reflecting one common way in which we do speak of beliefs and believing. If I say, 'I believe there is bread in the cupboard,' it would make sense for my wife to say, 'You'd better make sure.' Also, when I made my remark I was indicating my doubt and hesitancy. But if you hear a man testifying and saying, 'I believe in God,' you do not take this as an indication of hesitancy on his part. On the contrary, he might well be expressing one of his deepest convictions. By thinking

that the word 'belief' where religious beliefs are concerned is synonymous with conjecture or hypothesis,
Hirst violates the grammar of the concept in that context.[13] Wittgenstein recognized the importance of
noting that 'belief' is used differently in connection with
religious beliefs. He says that in religion 'One talks of
believing and at the same time one doesn't use "believe"
as one does ordinarily. You might say (in the normal
use): "You only believe – oh, well . . ." Here it is used
entirely differently; on the other hand it is not used as
we generally use the word "know".'[14]

Wittgenstein not only wants to separate religious
beliefs from the beliefs which are conjectures. He also
wants to show that they are different from what we
call knowledge. You cannot ask for a verification, an
external check, on religion as such. The difference
between those who do believe and those who do not is
not like the difference between two people with rival
hypotheses about the existence of a star. The people in
the latter disagreement disagree within a context common to both of them. But the difference between a
believer and a non-believer is a difference between
someone who does look on his life in a certain way and
regulates it accordingly and someone who has no time
for such a response or who sees nothing in it. Wittgenstein says that in religion 'believing obviously plays
much more this role: suppose we said that a certain
picture might play the role of constantly admonishing
me, or I always think of it. Here an enormous difference
would be between those people for whom the picture is
constantly in the foreground, and the others who just
didn't use it at all.'[15]

What of the question of truth in religion in the light

of the foregoing remarks? What follows from them, if they are accepted, is that whereas it makes sense to ask what is truly religious, it makes no sense to ask whether religion as such is true or false, if what one has in mind is an external non-religious or non-moral proof of the truth of religion. One can say that another religion is true or false where this statement is a religious or moral judgment. Professor Hirst should have recognized that 'truth' as used in connection with empirical statements is different from the notion of truth often used in religion, since he himself uses the word in both ways in his paper. An example of the first way of using 'truth' can be found in asking whether the statement that this road will get me to Swansea is true. Its truth depends on whether or not the road does in fact lead to Swansea. The road might have led me elsewhere. But Hirst also asks whether we have 'a domain of religious knowledge and truth'. Now, how is 'truth' being used here? I suggest that it is used in a way akin to that in which it is used when we say, 'There's a lot of truth in that,' or the way it was used when Jesus said, 'I am the way, the truth, and the life.' Here there is no question of an external check. If a person says, 'I have come to see the truth of the saying, that it is better to give than to receive,' and another person denies this, this is not like a dispute between business partners over whether a proposed venture will in fact materialize in profit. It is a dispute over the worth of generosity. And if someone has come to see the truth of it, that doesn't mean that he has assessed generosity by means of some measure other than generosity. What he has come to see is the beauty of generosity. When he says there is a lot of truth in it, what this comes to in practical terms is that he strives after it and tries to regulate his life accordingly. But while it is correct that to actually say that 'It is better to give than to receive' is to commit oneself to this view, it does not follow that this is why one thinks it is true. If someone asked one why one thought it was true, one would start talking, not about oneself or one's commitment, but about generosity.

I am suggesting that the ways in which the words 'truth' and 'true' can be used in connection with generosity is akin to the use of 'truth' in such utterances as 'God is Truth' or 'To love God is to know the truth'. So religious beliefs are not a class of second-best statements, hypotheses awaiting confirmation, or conjectures longing to be borne out. They are a body of truths, in the sense I have been talking about, which have played an important part in the history of mankind, and by which many people still regulate or attempt to regulate their lives.

If my arguments are correct I have now removed Hirst's main objections against teaching religion in schools. Hirst argued that religious beliefs are unconfirmed conjectures, matters of personal decision, with no objective standards of validity. On all these points, I have argued, he is mistaken.

But what are the implications of what I have said for the teaching of religion? First of all, it is quite clear that the questions I have raised in the philosophy of religion *are* raised by quite young children, and persist in more sophisticated forms throughout their school careers. In the sixth form, surely, such questions could be discussed in a philosophical manner. Students will be worried about the relations between religious statements and scientific statements, between religious beliefs and factual beliefs, between the notion of empirical truth and truth in religion, and so on. These questions, it seems to me, could and should be discussed, and there are obviously good educational reasons for doing so. These problems are real ones and form as real a part of enquiry as any other subject. I do not know whether one is going to call such discussion religious education or philosophy of religion, but that is not very important. Needless to say, these questions and an adequate discussion of them presuppose a historical knowledge of the religion in question. It seems that Professor Hirst would not object to this, since he does not think his arguments amount to saying that 'in maintained schools there ought not to be factual instruction about the beliefs that have played and do play so large a part in our history, literature, and way of life'.[16] Professor Hirst wants to distinguish between such instruction and advocacy, and I entirely agree with him on this matter. When I say that the notion of truth in religion should be elucidated, that is not the same as saying that it should be advocated. The reactions of children to such elucidation will probably be as varied as that of adults. But there are problems about Hirst's phrase 'factual instruction', since, as we have seen, elucidation of the nature of religious beliefs would involve showing the kind of beliefs they are, the role they play in people's lives, and so on. That will involve one inevitably in an elucidation of values and ideals, conceptions of worship and love. If Hirst is including all this within factual instruction, then I agree with him. If he is not, then the factual instruction will not achieve the desired elucidation.

Of course, there are problems about teaching religion

to younger children in the earlier classes. They could not indulge in the conceptual comparison and analysis I have said ought to go on in sixth forms. Yet I do not think that this rules out the possibility of the kind of elucidation I have been talking of. The problems made explicit by the sixth-former are present in varied forms in the younger child. The difficulty is that one cannot meet them by the same methods. I think they might be met, however, in the telling of stories. For example, the difference between a regard for generosity and a prudential outlook could be brought out in dramatic form. The child could be brought to see the difference between the two attitudes, how the emphasis differs in each. I see no reason for withholding the term 'elucidation' as a description of this activity. Again, such elucidation can be distinguished from advocacy.

I began this chapter with a plea to break down the polemical categories into which discussions of religious education tend to fall. The position I have taken up is in some ways similar to that of Simone Weil when she says:

> We perceive more clearly what justice demands in this matter, once the notion of right has been replaced by that of obligation to need. The soul of a child, as it reaches out towards understanding, has need of the treasures accumulated by the human species through the centuries. We do injury to a child if we bring it up in a narrow Christianity which prevents it from ever becoming capable of perceiving that there are treasures of the purest gold to be found in non-Christian civilizations. Lay education does an even greater injury to children. It covers up these treasures, and those of Christianity as well.[17]

Professor Hirst would agree, I think, on the desirability of teaching children something about the truths of other religions, but in answer to his worry that concentration on Christianity smacks of opportunism, Simone Weil would reply that 'as when studying history little French children are told a lot about France, so it is natural that, being in Europe, when you talk about religion you should refer primarily to Christianity'.[18]

Simone Weil says that ordering school-teachers to talk about God is a joke in extremely bad taste. But it is also foolish to assume a pseudo-neutrality like that of those mentioned in the *Gittins Report* who would say that 'religious education should be postponed until children are mature enough to be presented with the arguments for and against the Christian Faith and be able to decide whether they believe it or not'.[19] What are they going to decide about? The attitude expressed presupposes that in elucidating the nature of religious beliefs one would be advocating those beliefs, but as we have seen, the elucidation and the advocacy can be distinguished. I find what Simone Weil says about the question of the truth of what is taught far more penetrating. She says that

> One would talk about dogma as something which has played a role of the highest importance in our countries, and in which men of the very greatest eminence have believed wholeheartedly; without hiding the fact either that it has been the pretext for inflicting any number of cruelties. But, above all, one would try to make the children feel all the beauty contained therein. If they ask, 'Is it true?', we should answer: 'It is so beautiful that it must certainly contain a lot

of truth. As for knowing whether it is, or is not, absolutely true, try to become capable of deciding that for yourselves when you grow up.' It would be strictly forbidden to add, by way of commentary, anything implying either a negation of dogma or an affirmation of it.[20]

For Simone Weil the elucidation I talked of is the displaying of a thing of beauty. Whether the child regulates his life by this conception of beauty is something he will decide in later years. She stresses, however, that the stories are not to be dealt with as things of beauty to delight aesthetes. On the contrary, the study of religious texts, like the study of any texts, should always observe the spirit of the texts, and so stress their connection with the everyday world outside the school. For example, a rural school should pay particular attention to elucidating the meaning of the pastoral parables. In this way 'thought' and 'work' are no longer looked upon as being in watertight compartments. Simone Weil makes this point powerfully when she says that

> Naturally, a peasant who is sowing has to be careful to cast the seed properly, and not to be thinking about lessons learnt at school. But the object which engages our attention doesn't form the whole content of our thoughts. A happy young woman, expecting her first child, and busy sewing a layette, thinks about sewing it properly. But she never forgets for an instant the child she is carrying inside her. At precisely the same moment, somewhere in a prison workshop, a female convict is also sewing, thinking, too, about sewing properly, for she is afraid of being punished. One might imagine both women to be

doing the same work at the same time, and having
their attention absorbed by the same technical
difficulties. And yet a whole gulf of difference lies
between one occupation and the other.[21]

These remarks are extremely important as an answer to
those who would say that religious beliefs are irrelevant
to the wider context of a person's life.

If religious beliefs were elucidated in this way,
Simone Weil believes that it would abolish the polemical confrontation between two opposing camps, the
secular schoolmaster and the priest. She also thinks
that such a presentation of the content of religion 'would
imperceptibly imbue the mass of the population with
spirituality, if it is still capable of being so imbued'.[22]
I do not know whether this latter opinion is true. But
my point is that the case for teaching religion in schools
stands educationally and independently of this fact.
Not only is there a case for teaching religion because of
its content and the roles it has played and still plays in
human life, but also because of its connections with
other educational disciplines, the worth of which are
not in dispute. Simone Weil says that

It is too absurd for words that a French university
graduate should have read poetry of the Middle
Ages, *Polyeucte*, *Athalie*, *Phèdre*, Pascal, Lamartine,
philosophical doctrines impregnated with Christianity like those of Descartes and Kant, the *Divine
Comedy* or *Paradise Lost*, and never once have opened a
Bible. . . . An educational course in which no reference is made to religion is an absurdity.[23]

Professor Hirst says that religious education must
include 'the part played by Christian beliefs in deter-

mining our way of life'. It is hard, however, to make Hirst's argument consistent on these matters, since it is clear that he would not endorse the kind of comment I have quoted from the work of Simone Weil. He talks about the legitimacy of talking about an experience of mystery and contingency which may underlie all religion, but he does not want to talk about this in terms of any specific religious beliefs. But this recommendation is unintelligible. As far as a feeling of contingency is concerned, the feeling that we could be crushed at any moment, destroyed as persons, by external circumstances, that in itself is not a religious feeling. Religion enters when there is a certain response to that feeling. But that response need not be forthcoming, and the feeling of contingency may simply paralyse and terrorize a person. So to speak about a feeling of contingency is not necessarily to speak of religious beliefs at all. Secondly, contrast what Hirst says about the notion of mystery with the detailed elucidation of religious beliefs advocated by Simone Weil. I have no idea what an experience of mystery is which is not related to some context or other, for, after all, the intelligibility of the notion of experience depends on the context in which it is at work. A context-free concept of mystery would be mysterious indeed. After all, although conceptions of mystery are to be found in various religions, talk about mystery is not meant to be mysterious. Neither are the various criteria for the use of the conceptions in various religious traditions mysterious. So much more is needed than Hirst seems prepared to allow.

But at the close of his article, Hirst's argument takes yet another turn. Hirst sees hope in tendencies to explain religious beliefs as attempts to explain aspects of man's natural experience. He says that 'When it comes to tests for the truth of religious statements, the point must be the adequacy of the pictures in making sense of the range and circumstances of the experiences'.[24] This view has a superficial resemblance to the arguments advanced in this chapter, but there are important differences. Simone Weil stresses the role played by religious beliefs in daily life, but she does not suggest, like Hirst, that the beliefs are to be assessed by the facts in some sense or other. On the contrary, the religious beliefs are said to bring a characteristic emphasis to bear on the facts. The beliefs assess the facts, not the facts the beliefs.

In any case, Professor Hirst only sees these recent attempts to explain religion as the tentative beginnings of future possibilities. He says that 'perhaps this is just crystal-gazing', and that in 'the present state of affairs . . . philosophical considerations would seem to suggest'[25] that all we ought to have in religious education is the kind of thing he has argued for. I am suggesting, on the other hand, that the crystal in this case is the mistaken philosophical reasoning which has created the problems which Hirst tries to meet in his paper. Philosophical considerations in themselves show that religious education ought to be possible in schools; that there is something there to be elucidated and discussed.

Are we to say, then, that some kind of religious education *ought* to be given in schools? We may or we may not, but it is not a conclusion which *must* follow from the arguments of this chapter.[26] I have distinguished throughout between an elucidation of religious beliefs and an advocacy of them. The elucidation, nevertheless, calls for a sympathetic relation to religion in the teacher, since, as I said earlier, it involves unpacking the significance of values, ideals, different conceptions of worship and love, and the roles they play in people's lives. This is not a task confined necessarily to religious believers, but it is a task confined to those who take religion seriously, who see something in it, and respect it. This class of teachers could well include someone who had come to the conclusion that religious beliefs were false in that he had a regard in his own life for conflicting beliefs, but thought a great deal needed to be said to appreciate the nature of religious beliefs. Again, this class of teachers might well exclude someone who was a devout believer, but who lacked the ability to elucidate the nature of his beliefs. So the ability to teach in this context is not synonymous with the ability to believe; it is synonymous, however, with the ability to respect or to see something in religion. One might compare the case with that of musical education, which one equates, with good reason, with musical appreciation. It cannot be put in the hands of the tone deaf.[27] Because of the inseparability of understanding and sympathy where religious education is concerned, many might come to the conclusion that it is simply not possible to find such a condition satisfied sufficiently to feel confident about general provisions for religious education in schools. They might feel that religious education *should* be possible, but that in fact it is not. Compare, perhaps: 'People should be able to live in peace, but they don't.'[28] Others, despite the unlikelihood of the conditions for successful teaching of religious education being realized, might still think the risk worth taking, even if they have to supply a corrective themselves. The point to be made is that people may reach *different* conclusions concerning whether religious education ought in fact to be taught, *even when people agree that it should be possible to teach religious education.* Philosophical considerations as such cannot determine the evaluations people make. What such considerations do show is that it is possible to teach religion in schools, and that considerations which suggest the contrary, such as those advanced by Hirst, are based on conceptual confusions.

References

1. This paper was read to the Philosophy of Education Society of Great Britain at Bristol on 5 October 1968.
2. I was helped to see this with reference to Unamuno by Allen Lacy's stimulating study, *Miguel de Unamuno: the Rhetoric of Existence*, Mouton, 1967. I have reviewed this work in *Philosophical Quarterly*, 18, No. 71 (April 1968).
3. Hirst, Paul H., 'Morals, Religion, and the Maintained School', *British Journal of Educational Studies*, 14 (1965–6), 7.
4. *Ibid.*, 12.
5. *Ibid.*
6. *Ibid.*, 17–18.
7. *Ibid.*, 17.
8. 'The Terms of Ordinary Language are . . .' in *Philosophical Essays*, University of Nebraska Press, 1965, 205.
9. *Ibid.*, 204.
10. *Ibid.*, 206.
11. I have discussed these questions in ch. 7 of *The Concept of Prayer*, 'God's Voice and the Concept of Community', Routledge & Kegan Paul, 1965.
12. *Op. cit.*, 12.
13. Of course, sometimes religious beliefs are conjectures, e.g. 'I

believe this is the tomb of St Peter,' 'I believe in the authenticity of this holy relic,' etc.

14. Wittgenstein, Ludwig, *Lectures and Conversations on Aesthetics, Psychology, and Religious Belief*, ed. Barrett, Cyril, Basil Blackwell, 1966, 60.

15. *Ibid.*, 56.

16. *Op. cit.*, 13.

17. Weil, Simone, *The Need for Roots*, trans. Wills, A. F., Routledge & Kegan Paul, 1952, 87–8.

18. *Ibid.*, 88.

19. *Primary Education in Wales*, Dept. of Education and Science, H.M. Stationery Office, 1967, 367–8.

20. *Op. cit.*, 88–9.

21. *Ibid.*, 90–1.

22. *Ibid.*, 89.

23. *Ibid.*, 88.

24. *Op. cit.*, 17.

25. *Ibid.*, 17–18.

26. I have been helped to see this by some comments made by Professor R. F. Holland on an earlier version of this chapter.

27. Holland's example.

28. *Ibid.*

IX Wisdom's Gods

In this chapter I shall try to do two things: first, to expound Professor John Wisdom's writings on religion;[1] second, to raise questions as to the adequacy of the philosophical account of religion he provides. It may seem futile to expound writings which are available for all to read. I think I am justified in doing so, not only because of the complexity of the writings themselves, but also because through such an exposition, I hope to bring out aspects of Wisdom's arguments which have been virtually ignored by philosophers of religion.

PART ONE: EXPOSITION

I. *Why Philosophize About Religion?*
Sometimes, we not only ask questions, but ask questions about questions. We may do so because we are puzzled about how a word is being used in a question. For example, if someone asks, 'Is he your cousin?' we may be unclear about what question we are being asked, because we are unclear about how the word 'cousin' is being used. On the other hand, we may ask questions about questions because we are puzzled as to their general character. If we are asked whether it is criminal to do such-and-such, we may not know whether we are being asked a legal or a moral question. Or, if we are asked whether such-and-such ought to be done, we may not know whether we are to judge on moral grounds or

on grounds of expediency. In these cases we are hoping that the unknown will become known. But occasionally we ask questions about things that we know already. People ask, 'What is time?' although they know how to use the word 'time'. People are interested in questions about the nature of the past, although they can distinguish between the past and the future. They have asked, 'What is mind?' and 'What is matter?' These questions are metaphysical questions, and they are characteristic of philosophical enquiry (*RB* 44–5). These are the questions Wisdom is interested in. He wants to explore the logic of religious beliefs, and to discover what kind of question people are asking when they ask whether God exists.

Before embarking on this philosophical venture, however, it is well worth asking whether it is worth embarking on. There are two reasons which might dissuade us from undertaking the task. First, it has to be admitted that metaphysical speculation on the nature of certain questions has no influence on the task of answering those questions. No matter what conclusions the philosopher arrives at concerning the nature of the past, the historian goes on regardless (*RB* 45–6). In the second place, not only can metaphysical speculation have no influence on the answering of certain questions, but it can also distort and present a caricature of the questions which are to be answered. For example, as a result of metaphysical speculation on moral questions, some people have said that they are not real questions at all, since in 'answering' them men are simply saying, 'Do this sort of thing.' But is not this a caricature of moral questions? When a man asks of what he has done, ' "But *was* it all so right, so admirable?" ' isn't he wondering whether he hasn't been mistaken, blind? Doesn't he put all his mind with all his heart into trying to see things now, not as they then appeared, but more nearly as they were?' (*RB* 46).

Yet, despite these two reasons, Wisdom thinks that metaphysical speculation about religion is worthwhile and important. If there are two reasons for refraining from such speculation in this context, there are two better reasons for embarking on it. First, where religion is concerned, we must recognize that our metaphysical innocence is already lost. Things have already been said about the nature of religious beliefs which demand philosophical attention. For example, some people have said that we can accept statements about God without asking whether they are true or false or even without understanding them. But when people speak like this, do we not want to ask whether what *they* are saying is true? Wisdom certainly does:

For [he asks] how *can* one believe what one does not understand? How *can* one properly believe what one has not reason to believe? I am not saying that there is nothing to be said in answer to these questions. Words may come into a man's mouth and he may then say that he doesn't know what he meant by them. Later he may say, 'Ah! Now I see what I meant.' But all talk about 'believing what one doesn't understand' or 'having a right to believe what one has no reason to believe' needs careful explanation if one is to avoid 'all appearance of evil', the evil of saying what may seem to encourage confusion, superstition, and the determination of our beliefs by our desires (*RB* 48).

There are other people who have said that if religious questions are to be meaningful, and if religious beliefs are to tell us anything about what is the case, they must be capable of being settled by further experience, by experiments not yet carried out. Wisdom is also anxious to demonstrate the shortcomings and misunderstandings involved in this demand (*RB* 48).

The second reason why it is worthwhile to embark on metaphysical speculations concerning religious beliefs is because statements made about those beliefs, such as the two we have just considered, cannot be safely ignored. The observations are important in people's lives. They affect their hopes and fears, their frustrations and aspirations, and their understanding of themselves. Religious beliefs are among the most difficult to grasp. After an initial bewilderment we may cease to be puzzled by the existence of electrons. We may even come to see what is meant by someone who denies that life is driven by hate and a desire for power, and says that life is driven by an eternal longing for loyalty and affection. But these statements cannot be compared with the difficulty in understanding the religious statement, 'It may not seem so at first glance, but God knows it all and loves us still' (*RB* 49).

II. *Are Religious Beliefs Experimental Hypotheses?*

Why are religious statements so difficult to understand? The most obvious difficulty concerns their method of verification. Many religious statements seem to be making claims about what is the case, but it becomes obvious fairly soon that no observation can demonstrate the truth or falsity of the statements.

For instance, take an old question which has very much concerned people – the question 'Did Someone make the world?' 'Is there Someone behind it all?' This seems as if it could be answered like 'Who made this watch?' 'Who laid out this garden?' 'Is there a master mind behind all these seemingly disconnected crimes?' But it can't be answered in that way. It couldn't be. What I mean is this: when you are told that there is someone, God, who brings the young lions their prey and feeds the cattle upon a thousand hills, it is natural to think that if you watch, perhaps in the hush at dawn or at sunset, you will see something to confirm this statement. You watch. What d'you see? Antelopes feeding, perhaps, or zebras come down to drink. A lion springs – with wonderful acceleration it is true – but still his own acceleration. And if anything saves that zebra it's the way he comes round on his hocks and gets going. There are the stars and the flowers and the animals. But there's no one to be seen. And no one to be heard. There's the wind and there's the thunder, but if you call there's no answer except the echo of your own voice (*LG* 10–11).

No one among contemporary philosophers has done more than Wisdom to show us that religious beliefs are not experimental hypotheses about the world. Whenever this question is discussed nowadays, reference is likely to be made to Wisdom's parable of the long-neglected garden. We recall the difference of opinion which arose between two people revisiting such a garden. One man wanted to say that the garden afforded evidence of a gardener who came to the garden unseen and unheard, while the other man denied this.

Neither, however, observes any fact which the other does not observe. 'At this stage, in this context, the gardener hypothesis has ceased to be experimental, the difference between one who accepts and one who rejects it is now not a matter of the one expecting something the other does not expect' (*G* 155). Furthermore, we have reason to doubt whether any phenomenon, experimentally determined, could count as a demonstration of the existence of God. If we say that evidences in Nature afford proof of the existence of God, just as the existence of a watch or a house affords proof of the existence of a watchmaker and an architect respectively, we are still assuming that *God could* be seen.

Now what would it be like to see God? Suppose some seer were to see, imagine we all saw, move upwards from the ocean to the sky some prodigious figure which declared in dreadful tones the moral law or prophesied most truly – our fate. Would this be to see God? Wouldn't it just be a phenomenon which later we were able to explain or not able to explain, but in neither case the proof of a living God. This logic of God if there is such a logic isn't like that (*LG* 11).

What, then, should we say as philosophers about the nature of religious beliefs if we agree that they do not have the logical status of experimental hypotheses? Some philosophers have said that if we arrive at such agreement, we ought to be bold enough to say that religious beliefs are meaningless. These beliefs tell us nothing about what is the case, about how things are, and are incapable of verification or falsification. Other

175

philosophers, while agreeing that religious beliefs do not tell us anything about the world, deny that religious beliefs are meaningless. What these beliefs express are not matters which call for an investigation of the facts, but decisions on the part of believers, decisions to lead a certain way of life, and a commitment to certain policies of action. Wisdom is opposed to both of these philosophical groups, but he has more respect for the first than for the second. They, at least, were led to conclude that religious beliefs were meaningless out of a concern for the distinction between truth and falsity, whereas those who reduce religious beliefs to matters of decision have removed religious questions from the realms of truth and falsity, and by so doing have denied that they are real questions at all. Similar things have been said in other branches of philosophy – for example, in the philosophy of law. A philosopher of law might say that the arguments heard in a court of law when all the facts are known cannot be arguments about what is the case. Rather, he may suggest, we should regard such arguments as emotive means of bringing about a desired attitude or verdict.

But this won't do. It is of the essence of the law, not merely that justice be done, but that it be seen to be done. Neither legal enquiry nor moral enquiry is or could be a process in which, by hook or by crook, we induce an attitude and promote a policy. Argument must be heard. Argument which is not merely any psychological procedure which obtains a certain result, but a procedure in which we set this by that, and that by this, so as to see more plainly than we did at first what it was that happened, and then and only then to act. To describe such a procedure as a process primarily of persuasion to a line of action, to say that a search for the truth is not of the essence of this procedure, is to say what is dangerous, defamatory and false (*RB* 55).

Similarly, anyone who says that religious beliefs are not concerned with what in fact is so, although he is only making a statement about religious beliefs, and not a religious statement, may understandably be described as uttering ' "a blasphemous fable and a dangerous deceit" ' (*RB* 55). 'For it tries to take from the doctrines of religion, not merely something without which they would not *strictly* speaking be religious, but something without which they would no longer be themselves' (*RB* 55).

Wisdom is saying, then, that although in one sense all the facts may be known, in another sense questions involving a greater apprehension of the facts may remain. Many philosophers of religion have ignored this aspect of Wisdom's work. They have been content to conclude that since religious beliefs are not experimental hypotheses, they cannot tell us anything about what is so, about what is in fact the case. They have ignored the arguments Wisdom provides to show conclusively that this conclusion suffers from too narrow a conception of what is so and of what constitutes 'the facts'. Nor have philosophers been slow to use some of Wisdom's observations – for example, his parable of the long-neglected garden – to support their conclusions, despite the fact that, taken in context, these observations serve merely as the prelude to Wisdom's positive contributions to the determination of the logic of religious beliefs. As a result, Wisdom's philosophy of religion remains, at best, half-discussed.

III. *Religion and What is So*

Wisdom begins showing us how religious questions may be about what is so without being experimental hypotheses, by showing how this is possible with many non-religious questions. For example, we may get different answers to the same calculations. What is needed to settle the issue is not more facts, but a recount of the facts already before us. But this example may seem of little value in resolving theistic questions, since here we have a definite deductive procedure which will settle the issue. The same procedure will tell the accountant who has before him all the assets and liabilities of a firm whether that firm is solvent, and the statistician who has the records of births and deaths for the last fifty years whether the average man today has a greater expectation of life than he had twenty years ago (*LG* 6; *G* 156; *RB* 54). There are other questions, however, which cannot be answered in such a definite way. In a court of law, the facts agreed, questions may still arise as to whether a ledger is a document, whether a certain body is a public authority, whether reasonable care has been exercised, whether a certain action was negligent or not negligent, cruel or not cruel, whether a certain person was guilty or not guilty, mad or not mad (*G* 157; *LG* 7; *RB* 54). We might be tempted to think that there is no question of truth or falsity involved in such matters. They are matters for decision. They are resolved by a ruling by the judge. We see that 'the process of deciding the issue becomes a matter of weighing the cumulative effect of one group of severally inconclusive items against the cumulative effect of another group of severally inconclusive items' (*G* 157). We see too that this is not a matter 'of collecting from several inconclusive items of information an expectation as to something further, as when a doctor from a patient's symptoms guesses at what is wrong, or a detective from many clues guesses the criminal' (*G* 157–8). Yet, for all that, the decision is not arbitrary, for

> though the decision manifests itself in the application of a name it is no more merely the application of a name than is the pinning on of a medal merely the pinning on of a bit of metal. Whether a lion with stripes is a tiger or a lion is, if you like, merely a matter of the application of a name. Whether Mr So-and-so of whose conduct we have so complete a record did or did not exercise reasonable care is not merely a matter of the application of a name or, if we choose to say it is, then we must remember that with this name a game is lost and won, and a game with very heavy stakes (*G* 158; cf. *RB* 54–5 and *LG* 10).

Even though the resolution of legal questions may be more complex and harder to appreciate than the resolution of the questions which may face an accountant or a statistician, we may still feel that there are definite procedural limits within which they are to be settled. But there are other questions which tempt us to say that there can be no procedure for settling them. Yet, as Wisdom shows, these very questions illustrate why the line between the application of a name and the determination of the facts is not so easy to draw as this distinction might imply. So if we ask, 'What's in the application of a name?' the answer, as we have seen, may be 'Nothing' or 'Very much'. But Wisdom is anxious to point out that this 'Very much' has more than one source:

> suppose two people are speaking of two characters in a story which both have read or of two friends which both have known, and one says, 'Really, she hated him,' and the other says, 'She didn't; she loved him.' Then the first may have noticed what the other has not, although he knows no incident in the lives of the people they are talking about which the other doesn't know too, and the second speaker may say, 'She didn't; she loved him,' because he hasn't noticed what the first noticed, although he can remember every incident the first can remember. But then again he may say, 'She didn't; she loved him,' not because he hasn't noticed the patterns in time which the first has noticed, but because though he has noticed them he doesn't feel he still needs to emphasize them with 'Really, she hated him.' The line between using a name because of how we feel and because of what we have noticed isn't sharp. 'A difference as to the facts', 'a discovery', 'a revelation', these phrases cover many things (*G* 153-4; cf. *LG* 9).

But are we then to say that distinguishing love from hate or showing that what we took to be love is really hate or what we took to be hate is really love is a hopeless matter, beyond the scope of reason? The fact of the matter is that our practice shows that we do not believe such matters to be beyond the scope of reason. What is more, here too we have a technique, a procedure, though an informal one, for resolving the questions at hand. Wisdom calls this technique *the technique of connecting and disconnecting*. If we are trying to get someone to appreciate the beauty of a picture when he has said that he cannot see it, we not only ask him to look again at the picture as we re-emphasize its features, but we also compare it with other pictures, connecting features of the first with features of the others. But this connecting technique does not only apply to pictures. We apply it to actions too. Nathan brought out certain features of David's treatment of Uriah the Hittite by connecting them with the features of another story. Once he saw the connection, David's apprehension of what he had done was radically altered. And cannot the connecting technique be applied to love? We may feel that a lover's attitude to his beloved is crazy. He does not see her for what she is. He is blind to the way she is behaving. We may be able to bring him to see what is before him by connecting the actions of his beloved with similar ones in other contexts which have infuriated him. Thus we weaken his admiration and increase his understanding. Of course, this need not be the case. He may recognize all the analogies we draw and continue to love her. 'We then feel,' Wisdom says, 'that perhaps it is we who are blind and cannot see what he can see' (*G* 161). But, Wisdom adds – and I shall comment on the significance of this addition later – the fact that the lover continues to love in face of the connections his critic draws to his attention is not sufficient to show that his love is free from illusion. We draw the lover's attention, not only to connections which he may have missed, but also to connections which have, but should not have, influenced him. Our technique not only connects; it also disconnects. We are sometimes influenced by things which

Wisdom's Gods

should not influence us because of a mismanagement of
language, as when in the Monte Carlo fallacy a gambler
thinks that the probability of a number's turning up
increases with the length of time since its last appearance. But other influences on us which need to be
removed are more complex, since they are not expressed
in language at all. The task of disconnecting these
influences might be called 'reasoning to remove bad
unconscious reasoning' (G 162) or the work of sifting
causes from reasons. For example:

> suppose Miss Gertrude Stein finds excellent the work
> of a new artist while we see nothing in it. We
> nervously recall, perhaps, how pictures by Picasso,
> which Miss Stein admired and others rejected, later
> came to be admired by many who gave attention to
> them, and we wonder whether the case is not a new
> instance of her perspicacity and our blindness. But if,
> upon giving all our attention to the work in question,
> we still do not respond to it, and we notice that the
> subject-matter of the new pictures is perhaps birds in
> wild places and learn that Miss Stein is a bird-
> watcher, then we begin to trouble ourselves less about
> her admiration (G 163).

We have now moved from a consideration of the way
questions are resolved in the relatively straightforward
problems facing the accountant and the statistician,
through the resolution of questions which occur in a
law court, to questions which may arise in connection
with beauty, love, and hate. Wisdom suggests that the
logic of the divine can be accommodated by the complex aspects of this continuum. By stressing the techniques of connecting and disconnecting we may come to
see how ' "There is a God" . . . evinces some recognition

of patterns in time easily missed and that, therefore, difference as to there being any gods is in part a difference as to what is so and therefore as to the facts, though not in the simple ways which first occurred to us' (*G* 154). The parable of the long-neglected garden showed us that belief in God does not make a difference to our expectation of future happenings, and cannot be shown to be true or false experimentally. We then say that whether God exists makes no difference to the facts. This is true as far as it goes, but Wisdom is insisting that it does not follow from this that we can say of the question whether God exists that *'there is no right and wrong about it*, no rationality or irrationality, no appropriateness or inappropriateness, no procedure which tends to settle it, *nor even that this procedure is in no sense a discovery of new facts*' (*G* 159).

But Wisdom has to meet one more objection to this way of talking. Despite the subtleties of the techniques of connecting and disconnecting, it might be said that whereas we do know what to look for to count for or against the existence of energy, the nature of its transmission and conservation, and, though in different ways, what to look for to check on whether someone is pleased to see us or on whether what we took to be hate is really love, there is no agreement on what would count for or against the existence of God. But Wisdom does not believe this to be true: 'Not *no* agreement. If there were *no* agreement that *would* make the question meaningless' (*G* 16).

IV. *The Verifiability of Religious Beliefs*
How, then, are we to see what is meant by asking whether God or the Devil exist? Freud, in the last of his *New Introductory Lectures*, says:

It seems not to be the case that there is a Power in the universe which watches over the well-being of individuals with parental care and brings all their affairs to a happy ending. On the contrary, the destinies of mankind can be brought into harmony neither with the hypothesis of a Universal Benevolence nor with the partly contradictory one of a Universal Justice. Earthquakes, tidal waves, conflagrations, make no distinction between the virtuous and pious and the scoundrel or unbeliever. Even where an individual's fate depends on his relations to other people, it is by no means the rule that virtue is rewarded and that evil finds its punishment. Often enough the violent, cunning, or ruthless man seizes the envied good things of the world and the pious man goes away empty. Obscure, unfeeling, and unloving powers determine men's fate.[2]

'Obscure, unfeeling and unloving powers determine men's fate': do we not know what Freud meant?

It is not a modern theory but an old saying that in each of us a devil sleeps. Eve said: 'The serpent beguiled me.' Helen says to Menelaus:

> '. . . and yet how strange it is!
> I ask not thee; I ask my own sad thought,
> What was there in my heart, that I forgot
> My home and land and all I loved, to fly
> With a strange man? Surely it was not I,
> But Cypris there!'[3] (*G* 166; cf. *LG* 17).

There may be evasion and escapism in these words, but there is also truth in them. We do want to say that there are hidden powers of evil greater than ourselves within us and about us. By recognizing the reality of these powers we come to see what is meant by the existence of the Devil. On the other hand, we may feel that Freud is going too far when he says that obscure, unfeeling and unloving powers determine men's fate. For if there are hidden powers of evil within and about us, are there not also hidden powers of goodness? 'Elijah found that God was not in the wind, nor in the thunder, but in a still small voice. The kingdom of Heaven is within us, Christ insisted, though usually about the size of a grain of mustard seed, and he prayed that we should become one with the Father in Heaven' (*G* 167).

In the light of our discovery of these hidden powers of good and evil, what are we to say about the stories of the gods? Surely, a new aspect of the matter has now become clear to us. In trying to show misconnections in Miss Stein's artistic appreciation we may come to see connections we have missed. Similarly, with the case in question: 'Thinking to remove the spell exercised upon his patient by the old stories of the Greeks, the psycho-analyst may himself fall under that spell and find in them what his patient has found and, incidentally, what made the Greeks tell those tales' (*G* 163). We may begin by being interested in the origins of the belief in God:

What are our feelings when we believe in God? They are feelings of awe before power, dread of the thunderbolts of Zeus, confidence in the everlasting arms, unease beneath the all-seeing eye. They are feelings of guilt and inescapable vengeance, of smothered hate and of a security we can hardly do without. We have only to remind ourselves of these feelings and the stories of the gods and goddesses and heroes in which these feelings find expression, to be reminded of how we felt as children to our parents and the big people of our childhood. . . . When a man's father fails him by death or weakness how much he needs another father, one in the heavens with whom is 'no variableness nor shadow of turning' (*G* 164–5).

If we remained here, we might write off the stories of the gods as understandable fabrications:

But here a new aspect of the matter may strike us. For the very facts which make us feel that now we can recognize systems of superhuman, sub-human, elusive, beings for what they are – the persistent projections of infantile phantasies – include facts which make these systems less fantastic. What are these facts? They are patterns in human reactions which are well described by saying that we are as if there were hidden within us powers, persons, not ourselves and stronger than ourselves (*G* 166).

We are thus brought to see that the realities expressed in stories about the gods are still with us. 'The Greeks did not speak of the dangers of repressing instincts, but they did speak of the dangers of thwarting Dionysos, of neglecting Cypris for Diana, of forgetting Poseidon for Athena. We have eaten of the fruit of a garden we can't forget, though we were never there' (*G* 167). By the patient technique of connecting and disconnecting, often with the aid of investigation by observation, we can throw light on these patterns of human reactions which express the reality of our belief in gods. In this way, by this complex route, Wisdom claims to have shown that 'the old questions, "Does God exist?" "Does the Devil exist?" aren't senseless, aren't beyond the scope of thought and reason. On the contrary, they call for a new awareness of what has so long been about us, in case knowing nature so well we never know her' (*LG* 22).

PART TWO: CRITICISM

I. *Is Wisdom Discussing Religion?*

Professor Wisdom is the declared enemy of scepticism. If anything claims to be knowledge, there must be a right and wrong about it; it must not be beyond the scope of reason. The same is true of the claim to know God. Wisdom says that he is 'not trying to prove that God does exist, but only to prove that it is wrong to say that there could be no proof that He does or that He does not' (*LG* 14). Still, in showing the kind of proof statements about God are subject to, it is difficult not to reveal at the same time the kind of reality we believe God must have if His existence is asserted or denied. This is certainly true of Wisdom's analysis of religious beliefs. If we find his notion of how God's existence might be proved inadequate, we are likely to conclude that his notion of God is inadequate too.

We might think that in some respects Wisdom's account of religion resembles Manichaeism. He stresses again and again the powers of goodness and the powers of evil that war within us and about us. How could he reach any other conclusion once he had said that the reality of supernatural beings was to be located in certain 'patterns in human reactions which are well described by saying that we are as if there were hidden

187

within us powers, persons, not ourselves and stronger than ourselves'? (*G* 166). Who can deny that some of these powers are good and that others are evil? 'Indeed, what makes us speak of the unconscious and the good and the evil in it . . . is closely connected with what makes us speak of a hidden power for good – God – and a hidden power for evil – the Devil' (*LG* 18).

Now, the fact that there are some affinities between Wisdom's account of religion and a well known heresy is not a philosophical criticism of that account. Nevertheless, it does suggest at least that Wisdom's account of religious statements is not the only possible account. I shall not concern myself with the account he gives of the Greek gods, but as far as his account of Christian and Hebrew beliefs are concerned, I shall argue that Wisdom's account is, not simply not the only possible one, but in fact mistaken. Before attempting to do so, however, I ought to point out that I am not denying that there may be people for whom religion means the kind of thing Wisdom has been talking about. Are we then to say that Wisdom has been discussing religion? Here we may feel like asking, 'What's in the application of a name?' The answer, as when Wisdom asked the question, is 'Nothing' or 'Very much.' If there are people who, like Wisdom, want to call certain patterns of human reactions 'religion', whether we allow them to do so is simply a matter of the application of a name. But, clearly, Wisdom has more in mind than this. He is not claiming to be describing an idiosyncratic or eccentric kind of religion. On the contrary, Wisdom claims to be showing the way in which we can set about proving whether God exists, to ignore which is to ignore what is of the essence of religion. So very much is involved in whether we apply the name 'religion' to what Wisdom is describing, for if we do we are agreeing that Wisdom is giving an account of the essence of religion. Such agreement would be a mistake. My reason for thinking so can be illustrated by five inter-related criticisms.

II. *The Reality of God and Patterns in Human Reactions*

First, let us examine the context Wisdom wishes to ascribe to the Christian concepts of hope, thanksgiving, love, etc. He thinks of them in terms of the patterns which can be found in certain human reactions. But other patterns are also present: those expressed in hate, strife, envy, malice, and the like. Would it not be a form of blindness or escapism to stress one set of patterns and ignore the other?

> Many have tried to find ways of salvation. The reports they bring back are always incomplete and apt to mislead even when they are not in words, but in music or paint. But they are by no means useless; and not the worst of them are those which speak of oneness with God. But in so far as we become one with Him He becomes one with us. St John says He is in us as we love one another. This love, I suppose, is not benevolence, but something that comes of the oneness with one another of which Christ spoke. Sometimes it momentarily gains strength. Hate and the Devil do too. And what is oneness without otherness? (*G* 168).

For Wisdom, giving thanks for life as such or hating life as such are equally mistaken, since is not life a mixture of good and evil which demands love where love is due and hate where hate is due? It appears that our great need is to appreciate the nature of this complexity, and by so doing strive to increase the good at the expense of the evil.

No one would deny that a person's salvation may lie in his freeing himself from self-deception. William Faulkner, in his *Sanctuary* and *Requiem for a Nun*, illustrates, through the character of Temple Drake, the need to see oneself as one really is. Temple's trouble was that she could not see her life in any kind of perspective; she could not see the bearing which one event had on another. Her salvation consisted largely in coming to understand the truth about herself. For most Christians, however, such an understanding would still leave one on the threshold of religion. For them, faith in God does not seem to be simply the recognition of the hidden good there is in life, but a mode of accepting or responding to the good and evil there is in life. Wisdom can give no account of this response to *the whole* of life, the acceptance of the complex patterns of human reactions, since he has already identified statements about God with a *limited number* of these reactions. I am suggesting that such an identification falsifies the character of some central religious views of life. For example, those who give thanks for life *whatever is the case* seem blind to Wisdom.[4]

They often speak of God's unfailing love and of His tremendous power, in spite of all the wretchedness in the world, the misery that is apparent and the misery that is hidden. Are they blind? Are they crazy? Of course, they do not deny that there have been famines, pestilence, wars. But after all, a man can admit all these and yet never really see, never realize what has gone on and does go on – until perhaps something happens which brings it home to him (*RB* 49–50).

But what is Wisdom going to say about the Christian claim that it is to the whole of life, to the good and the evil in it, that God brings salvation from despair? His philosophy of religion does not allow him to say anything about it. We are judged, according to Wisdom, on the basis of the facts about us. The only difference between divine judgment and human judgment is that the former is free from limitations, and is thus able to provide a correct analysis of the facts:

> But though we do make and need to make limited judgments we need again and again to call to mind how different they are from the divine judgment in which both easy forgiveness and easy condemnation are impossible. This is the judgment we ask for ourselves. For we ask that at our own trial counsel and judge shall proceed with infinite patience. We ask that they shall not judge a part of the picture without seeing the whole. We ask that they shall consider, ruthlessly but with understanding, circumstance beyond circumstance, wheel within wheel (*F* 33).

But what if the picture, the final picture, is black rather than white? Presumably the verdict then is 'Guilty'. This seems a far cry from the God who loved man *whilst he was yet a sinner*. Here, the possibility of being forgiven by God does not depend on the good in one outweighing the evil. If God were only relevant to the good in a man's life He could not bring hope or salvation to it.

For Wisdom, the correct analysis of the facts about us in the divine judgment is an unattainable ideal. But when Christians say of someone, 'What a pity he doesn't believe,' they are not saying, 'What a pity the good in him does not outweigh the evil,' 'What a pity he doesn't improve,' or 'What a pity he is not as we are.' They are saying, 'What a pity he doesn't see that, though he is a sinner, he can still walk with God.' For the Christian this refers, not to an unattainable ideal, but to a present reality.

I realize, of course, that much more needs to be said about what is meant by 'walking with God'. I certainly do not want to suggest that anything a believer says is intelligible simply because he says it. I think, however, that sense *can* be found in the idea of salvation I have outlined, but to elaborate further on it would be to embark on too long a story to relate here.[5] What I hope I have illustrated in this first criticism of Wisdom is the obvious incongruity between his analysis of religious statements and certain beliefs which are fundamental in Christianity.

III. *Religious Beliefs as Non-experimental Hypotheses*

Because Wisdom holds that the reality expressed by beliefs about God are to be found in certain patterns of human reactions, those beliefs are for him, at best, hypotheses. This is the second objection to his analysis of religious statements. Although they are not experimental hypotheses, the truth of religious beliefs is dependent on what happens to be the case about human reactions. As we have seen, beliefs about God are said to refer to patterns in time which are easily missed. These patterns are clarified by the techniques of connecting and disconnecting which we have already discussed. But do Christians speak of their beliefs about God as hypotheses which may or may not be true? It seems pretty clear that they do not. Their beliefs are absolutes for them.

Wisdom says:

> When St Paul said, 'The wages of sin is death,' he said what, though it is not obviously true, is yet something which, to say the least, may be true. It involved a moral judgment and it involved also an assertion as to what happens. . . . The words 'If ye forgive not men their trespasses, neither will your Father forgive your trespasses' (Matt. vi.15) seem to convey a warning. The words 'If ye forgive men their trespasses your heavenly Father will also forgive you' seem to convey a hope. Whether or not the hope is false or unfounded, it was hope they were intended to convey (*RB* 55–6).

Wisdom intends these examples to be evidence for his thesis that religious beliefs have to do with what in fact is the case. But when he says that it *may* be true that the wages of sin is death, and that the hope of one's own forgiveness if one has forgiven others may be false or unfounded, Wisdom betrays a misunderstanding of these religious beliefs. He speaks as if their truth were a matter of factual enquiry. It reminds one of the way Polus misunderstood Socrates's statement that good actions are always advantageous to the agent. Polus thought that the goodness of the action was one thing; its advantage a further item. Thus the refutation of Socrates was thought to be an easy matter. All that was needed was to point to a happy Archelaus, to one evil man who flourished or one good man who came to grief. But, of course, this did not refute Socrates. Socrates was saying that one must have a love of the good to see the good as advantageous, and a hatred of evil to see the bad as disadvantageous. The greatest plight to be in is not to recognize this. Similarly, to see that the wages of sin is death one must have a horror of sin. But Wisdom speaks as if sin were one thing and its wages another. Many have spoken in the same way, as if one did not sin because of supernatural sanctions, and one pursued the good for the sake of supernatural rewards. We could then raise the question of whether the sanctions or the rewards are real or what we took them to be. But why should we think that any of this would tell us anything about the religious beliefs Wisdom mentions? Would the fear of punishment or the hope of reward bring us to see what is meant by the horror of sin or the love of God? Similarly, when Wisdom speaks of the hope and the warning connected with divine forgiveness, he speaks as if a person's forgiveness of others is one thing and God's forgiveness another thing which may or may not follow. Kierkegaard comments on such views:

> Truly this is a misunderstanding. Christianity's view is: forgiveness *is* forgiveness; your forgiveness is your forgiveness; your forgiveness of another is your own forgiveness; the forgiveness which you give you receive, not contrariwise that you give the forgiveness which you receive.[6] It is as if Christianity would say: pray to God humbly and believing in your forgiveness, for he really is compassionate in such a way as no human being is; but if you will test how it is with

respect to the forgiveness, then observe yourself. If honestly before God you wholeheartedly forgive your enemy . . . then you dare hope also for your forgiveness, for it is one and the same. God forgives you neither more nor less nor otherwise than *as* you forgive your trespassers. It is only an illusion to imagine that one himself has forgiveness, although one is slack in forgiving others. . . . It is also conceit to believe in one's own forgiveness when one will not forgive, for how in truth should one believe in forgiveness if his own life is a refutation of the existence of forgiveness![7]

It is possible, as Kierkegaard shows, to enquire as to whether forgiveness is present or not. It would be possible too to show the results of the presence of envy in the soul. But this would not be the testing of a hypothesis, but an illustration of the presence of envy in life.

IV. *Religion and Justification*

Why does Wisdom regard religious beliefs as hypotheses? Partly, it has to do with his desire to show that religious beliefs are justifiable. His aim is not to justify them or refute them, but to show them to be the kind of beliefs which can be justified or refuted. This brings us to a third criticism that can be made of Wisdom's philosophy of religion. His account of the justification of religious beliefs suffers from an unresolved ambiguity. Wisdom confuses the question whether there can be a justification of an individual's claims regarding religious beliefs with the question whether there can be a general justification of religious beliefs. The difference between these questions can be brought out in terms of two examples we have already discussed.

First, consider the difference between two comments on a human relationship, one person saying, 'Really, she hated him' and the other saying, 'She didn't; she loved him.' Wisdom tells us that this difference may exist, although each person appeals to the same incidents in the relationship as the other does. The difference is a difference of emphasis, a difference in the patterns discerned in the incidents, and therefore a difference in the apprehension of the facts. Wisdom claims that it makes sense here to raise the question whether saying 'Really, she hated him' or 'She didn't; she loved him' is true or false, appropriate or inappropriate. Similarly, in the second example, Wisdom claims that it makes sense to ask whether the lover's attitude to his beloved is appropriate or not, whether he is blind to what others can see. The truth or falsity, appropriateness or inappropriateness, blindness or clear-sightedness, are said to be brought out partly by the patient technique of bringing out hidden connections.

But is it always possible to prove, or reason, something as 'the answer', even in disagreements on specific religious questions?[8] If one man says a person's belief is shallow and another person denies this, is there much one can do here? One person may get the other to see patterns he has missed. That *may* happen. But in many cases deadlock is soon reached, and that is that. Wisdom says:

> If I say of a cat, 'This cat is an abracadabra,' I utter a senseless string of words. I don't make a statement at all, and therefore don't make an absurd statement . . . the words, 'In Nero God was incarnate', are not without any meaning; one who utters them makes a

statement, he makes a statement which is absurd and *against* all reason and therefore *not* beyond the scope of reason. . . . 'In Jesus God was incarnate' is logically parallel to 'In Nero God was incarnate'. The latter we noticed is not beyond the scope of reason. There- fore the statement 'In Jesus God was incarnate' is not beyond the scope of reason (*LG* 20).

But would Nero think it absurd to say that in Nero God was incarnate? Would many of his contemporaries have thought it absurd to say so? Would it be absurd to say that in a cat God was incarnate?[9] Think of sacred animals. Again, think of the disputes surrounding Jesus. Did He or did He not fulfil the prophecies? It is extremely difficult for us now to grasp the force which the appeal to Scriptural authority or the authority of miracles had. In any case, to speak of fulfilment of prophecy begs the question, since there was no general agreement on what counts as fulfilment. Wisdom also speaks of the appropriateness or inappropriateness of certain reactions. But whose reactions has he in mind, mine or the mystic's, for example?[9] These reactions will certainly be different, but what does it mean to speak of appropriateness or inappropriateness here?

It does not follow from the above examples that we *never* have grounds for doubt and denial where religious beliefs are concerned. If John says that he is a deeply religious man and yet seems to have no interest in religious matters, or not to care one way or the other in situations where we would expect his beliefs to deter- mine what he says and does, we will conclude that John is not deeply religious after all. St Paul said that spirits must be discerned to see whether they are of God.

Beliefs which claim to be genuine may turn out to be
confused, shallow, hypocritical, or false. Tolstoy shows
us how Father Sergius came to see that what he took to
be the service of God was in fact the service of man, and
how he also saw that Pashenka, who thought she was
serving men, was in fact serving God. When one thinks
of the ways in which pride and humility may be interwoven in a man's life, one may see how complex a form
mistakes can take in religion. In all these examples,
there is a difference between what seems to be the case
and what in fact is the case, between illusion and
reality. But what has to be remembered is that all these
examples referred to the specific beliefs of individuals.
Questions of appropriateness or inappropriateness may
arise in other ways at this level. Bonhoeffer did not
think it appropriate to utter words of Christian comfort
to a normally frivolous fellow prisoner of war who was
breaking down during a heavy bombing raid. He
simply said, 'It won't last more than ten minutes now.'
Confronted by a bleeding body in a ditch, one might
say that the appropriate thing to do was not to think
about God, but to think about the bleeding body. But
again we are considering specific cases. The danger is
to think that one can move from these to ask in general
whether religious beliefs are true or false, appropriate or
inappropriate.

Wisdom wants to enquire into '*the reasonableness, the pro-
priety of belief in gods*' (*G* 163). But what does this mean?

What Wisdom says about a general justification of
beliefs is rather obscure, as we shall see in a moment,
but he does seem to think that the technique of connecting may serve this purpose. Here is his example:
'Imagine that a man picks up some flowers that lie half-

withered on a table and gently puts them in water. Another man says to him, "You believe flowers feel." . . . The Sceptic says, "You believe flowers feel," because something about the way the other man lifts the flowers and puts them in water suggests an attitude to the flowers which he feels inappropriate, although perhaps he would not feel it inappropriate to butterflies' (*G* 160). The inappropriateness of the attitude to flowers (though there may be deadlock on this issue) is brought out in this case by comparing it with examples of care being shown in other contexts. But can this be done where God's care is concerned? What other kinds of care similar in kind could it be compared with? Perhaps there are limited analogies with a father's care for his children, but one uses these analogies to hint at the meaning of God's care, not to prove its appropriateness. In any case, would Wisdom say it made sense to ask why we should care for people *at all*?

Wisdom is seeking justifications beyond the point where it makes sense to do so. Where loving God or loving people are concerned, ultimately, it is not a question of our seeking proofs of the appropriateness and truth of the love, but of our being won over by the love, and the love becoming our criterion of truth and appropriateness. It is not the believer who assesses the love of God, but the love of God that assesses the believer.

The unresolved ambiguity in Wisdom's argument is well illustrated by his own example:

People say, 'A man should stand up for himself.' Alexy Alexandrovitch in Tolstoy's *Anna Karenina* felt society contemptuous of him because he did not take more vigorous action against his wife and Vronsky.

199

On the other hand, there are those who insist that we should be tolerant not seven times, but seventy times seven. But even among those who set very high the limits of proper tolerance few will deny that there are limits; nearly all will allow that some insults, some injuries to oneself, call for some measure of resistance, even violent measures. But now that we have recalled the occasions when tolerance is false, or foolish, or unfair to others or unfair to oneself, we may remember those who have urged that a certain inward tolerance is, even in extreme cases, not out of place (*T* 141).

Wisdom then mentions Christ's words of forgiveness on the Cross and comments: 'We do not regard Christ's tolerance as false or out of place. We do not think it was achieved at the price of deceiving Himself about human beings' (*T* 141). Wisdom evades the issue here, since to show that Christ was not deceived by the motives of those who had crucified or deserted him is not the same as giving some kind of justification of his words of forgiveness. I do not know what such a 'justification' would be.

V. *Religion and Scepticism*

Why does Wisdom stress the necessity for justification so much? The answer is to be found in the measures he thinks one must take to overcome scepticism. Wisdom admits that even when the technique of connecting has done its utmost, unity of judgment need not be forthcoming. In the dispute we have mentioned between the person who says, 'Really, she hated him,' and the other who says, 'She didn't; she loved him,' the second may recognize all the patterns in time recognized by the first, but still not feel the need to emphasize those patterns with 'Really, she hated him.' The lover may see all his critic sees, but continue to love. What Wisdom says about these cases is obscure, since they are rather played down. I shall therefore put my fourth objection in the form of a question. Is there a possibility of justifying emphases, of saying which emphasis is right and which is wrong, when all patterns and hidden connections are known? Does Wisdom think that if the technique of connecting goes on long enough with sufficient patience eventual agreement will be forthcoming? Will we all agree on the artistic merits of Tolstoy or Picasso? Will all moral disagreements be resolvable? Will we know whether God exists or not once and for all? Wisdom's stress on the facts, on what is so, suggests that he would answer these questions in the affirmative. Unless agreement is reached in these spheres, Wisdom seems to think that there is no right and wrong, truth or falsity, about the matters involved. But in order to refute scepticism about art, morality, and religion, one does not need to show that people *agree* on all artistic, moral, and religious questions. What needs to be shown is that there is a real difference between the presence and absence of artistic, moral, and religious considerations.

VI. *Reasons and Causes*

There is one piece of evidence which suggests that my fourth criticism is not unfair. When Wisdom admits that the lover may continue to love despite the fact that the connections between his beloved's actions and other actions which have annoyed him have now been recognized by him, he says, 'We may then feel that it is we who are blind' (*G* 161). But he adds significantly that before we admit our inadequacy we must also look for misconnections in the lover's love. We must see that he has not been influenced by bad unconscious reasoning. We must sift the lover's reasons from the causes operating on him. Wisdom says that 'such is our confidence in the light of reason' (*G* 161). Few of us would be happy with the implication in Wisdom's argument – namely, that in a deadlock on moral or religious questions, if we are not the victims of bad unconscious reasoning and hidden causal forces, those who disagree with us must be.

For Wisdom, trust in reason does seem to imply that ultimate agreements can be reached. The question he must answer, however, is whether if one man says, 'There is a God,' and another says, 'There is no God,' or if one man loves God and another hates him, can it be the case when all relevant observations have been made, all patterns in time made explicit, all bad unconscious reasoning and hidden causes investigated and purged, that one man's love of God will remain as constant as the other's hate or denial? Wisdom is committed to saying that this could not be the case because of his unitary conception of 'what is so' and 'the facts'.

VII. *Conclusions*

Wisdom delivers us from the mistakes of a positivism which insists on seeing religious beliefs as experimental hypotheses. He shows us the greater complexity involved in what constitutes a fact, what is so, or a proof. But he does not go far enough. Ironically, though Wisdom began by criticizing a too narrow view of these concepts, in the end his own philosophy of religion comes under the same judgment.

I do not deny the reality of Wisdom's gods. They may be within us and about us. But I do deny that they represent the essence of religion, or what is most important in Hebrew and Christian religion. When Wisdom's account is over, we are still merely on the threshold of the Faith proclaimed in those traditions.

References

1. In this chapter I shall refer to five papers by Wisdom: 'Gods', as reprinted in *Philosophy and Psychoanalysis*, Basil Blackwell, 1953; 'The Logic of God', 'Religious Belief', 'Freewill', and 'Tolerance', as reprinted in *Paradox and Discovery*, Basil Blackwell, 1965. I shall refer to the papers in the text by the initials *G, LG, RB, F* and *T*, respectively, the number following the intitials being the page reference of the appropriate volume.

2. Freud, Sigmund, *New Introductory Lectures on Psychoanalysis*, Lecture XXXV, 'The Question of a *Weltanschauung*', *Complete Psychological Works of Sigmund Freud*, trans. Strachey, James, Hogarth Press, 1964 (1932–6), 167.

3. Euripides, *The Trojan Women*, trans. Murray, Gilbert.

4. There is an example I consider later which counts against this assertion. See pp. 201–2.

5. I have tried to tell this story in *The Concept of Prayer*. See ch. 5 where I discuss prayers of confession and the sense of saying that one can be forgiven *despite the person one is*, and ch. 6, where I discuss prayers of thanksgiving and the sense of giving thanks for one's life *whatever is the case*.

6. Contrast this with Wisdom's remark about the patience of divine judgment: 'Asking for this patience for ourselves, we then ask it for others and so ask it of ourselves' (*F* 33).

7. Kierkegaard, Sören, *Works of Love*, trans. Hong, Howard and Edna, Collins, 1962, 351–2.

8. I am indebted in the treatment of this question to the discussion of my paper at the Philosophical Society of the University College of Swansea.

9. I owe these examples to Mr Rush Rhees.

X Subjectivity and Religious Truth in Kierkegaard

When I talk about Kierkegaard to many Catholics, what they seem disturbed by most is Kierkegaard's coupling of subjectivity and truth.[1] Many people, when they read Kierkegaard, are disturbed by the same thing. And, at first, it does seem odd to speak of subjectivity and truth in the same breath. Surely, what should be coupled is not subjectivity and truth, but objectivity and truth. What is true must be objective, it must be public, it must admit of an external check. These are the hallmarks of knowledge and truth. When we speak of subjectivity, something very different comes to mind: we speak, not of knowledge and truth, in this context, but of opinion, conjecture, or belief. Unlike knowledge, belief or opinion does not require an external check; it is not public, but private. These differences can be illustrated very simply. If I say now, 'I know that the University College of Swansea is still standing,' I could be shown to be wrong. Since I left Swansea, a fire may have broken out on the campus and completely destroyed the College. If that were true, what do I have to say about my claim that I knew that the University College of Swansea was still standing? I have to say that I was wrong. I thought I knew, but in fact I did not. Here we have an important distinction between what I said and what in fact was the case. It doesn't follow that I know something because I say I know it: there must be an external check on the claim to know. But if, instead of saying that I know that the University College of Swansea is still standing, I say that I believe that the College is still standing, the consequences differ. If it turned out that the College had been destroyed by fire, it would not follow that I did not believe otherwise. Although what I believed was false, I did believe it. But if what I claimed to know turns out to be false, then I did not know it. Beliefs can be true or false, but 'false knowledge' is a contradiction in terms.

Now if we ask Christians how they think of the reality of God, many of them will insist that it does not depend on the assertions of an individual. They believe that this reality constitutes truth, and truth is something an individual can be right or wrong about; it certainly is not established because an individual says it is established. Certainly, Catholics would want to emphasize these points. Truth, they would want to say, has nothing to do with subjectivity; it has an objectivity found in the Scriptures, in history, and in the teachings of the Church. To say that subjectivity is truth is to tread the most dangerous of paths: to found eternal truth on individual emotion and conjecture. Such emotionalism and individualism must be avoided at all costs. Man's salvation is to be found, not in his own conjectures, but in the objective truth presented by the Church.

These are some of the reactions to Kierkegaard, or what they have heard about Kierkegaard, that I have found to be quite common among Catholics. I do not know, of course, how many people reading this paper

share the misgivings I have mentioned, but I should be
very surprised if no one did. It was against this background that I decided to devote this paper to the theme
of subjectivity and truth. It is so easy to misunderstand
and distort what Kierkegaard wishes to emphasize. I
may not succeed in getting you to agree with Kierkegaard, but I shall be content if I am able to rescue a
small part of what he says from some current misunderstandings.

To understand what Kierkegaard was trying to get at
in saying that truth is subjectivity, we need to pay attention to a contrast he draws again and again in what
many regard as his most important work, the *Concluding
Unscientific Postscript*.[2] The contrast I refer to is the one
Kierkegaard draws between the world-historical and
the subjective. He speaks of this contrast in discussing
the nature of the believer's ethical relationship to God.
The believer who moves from the world-historical to the
subjective, has, according to Kierkegaard, bridged an
infinite gulf – or, better, has leapt over an infinite gulf,
since there is no rational bridge which can be built
from the world-historical to the subjective. This is
because the difference between them is not one of
degree but of kind. When one moves from the world-
historical to the subjective a radical transition is
involved: a transition from the quantitative to the
qualitative.

Kierkegaard asks a number of questions in the *Postscript*: What does it mean to die? What does it mean to
be married? What does it mean to thank God for the
good He has bestowed upon one?[3] Now, these questions
can be posed and answered at two levels: the world-
historical level or the objective level, and the subjective

level. The objective answers to the questions are obvious enough. We know a great deal about death. We may have witnessed the deaths of many people, even of those who were dear to us. We know that death is the lot of all men. We also know a great deal about the causes of death. There may be some measure of medical disagreement about the definition of death – for example, whether only cellular death is to count as death. But these are problems which will be tackled according to the needs of medicine, according to what can and cannot be done to prolong life, or to provide spare parts for the human body. But the question of death can arise at another level. It can be raised in connection with the meaning of life. And on this level, what you find out about death, the conclusions you reach, will not be something in which you may or may not show any interest. You do not arrive at a series of objective facts. What you arrive at determines your whole attitude to life, whether your life has been worthwhile or not. The unavoidability of death may make one's life of planning and ambition seem a mockery and foolishness. But to come to see this is to have an ethical relationship to death which is not based on the objective facts we mentioned earlier. It is not a conclusion which can be deduced or inferred from them. It is a way of assessing or emphasizing the facts, and this way is not itself an additional fact.

But, of course, there are ways of assessing and emphasizing the facts which remain on the level of the objective. A marriage may be assessed in this way. Whether one is married is a legal question which admits of a legal answer. Whether the marriage is a success may be assessed in terms of whether it has furthered the plans a person had in mind when he married. People might say, 'She has been a great asset to him,' or they might say, 'He would have got somewhere if it hadn't been for her.' This is the objective method of assessment: it looks for consequences and effects. It praises well-conceived steps taken towards rationally determined ends. But marriage can be viewed in another way. It can be viewed subjectively. One might be forced to see that although one is married in the eyes of the law, one's marital relationship is nothing but a form of prostitution. Or, again, instead of assessing the marriage in terms of what one can get by it, the possibilities of attainment may be judged in the light of the marriage vows. Two people may be presented with prospects of success, and yet refuse them because they know what they would become if they went that way. For them, what they are to become is not determined by the prospects that come their way, but rather the prospects which come their way are judged by what they have vowed to be. This is one reason for saying that the prospects are temporal, but the vows are eternal.

The Christian, Kierkegaard wants to say, is aware of this distinction between the eternal and the temporal. He may not be able to give a philosophical account of the distinction, but that does not matter, for the marks of his understanding are not shown in his intellect, but in his life. They are shown, for example, in the way he thanks God for all the good He has bestowed upon him. Such thanksgiving is easily misunderstood. If it is understood in the world-historical sense, it is distorted out of all recognition. A man will decide whether he has anything to thank God for by totting up the pros and cons. Whether thanks is given will depend on how the weeks go by. Some weeks will be better than others. Such a man will not see that God has any necessary claims on him. Thanking God, for him, is a contingent, not a necessary, activity. It depends on the outcome, on how things go; it is dependent on the world-historical, as Kierkegaard would say. Such a believer, if he knew any philosophy, would say that non-Christian philosophers like Professor Antony Flew,[4] and Christian philosophers like Professor John Hick, are perfectly right in saying that if 'God loves mankind' is to mean anything, it must make a difference to the course of a man's life and to the course of other people's lives: life must go in one direction rather than another – which direction is unspecified. Kierkegaard would not agree with them. He sees, rightly, that thanking God is a necessity, not an option, for the Christian. How is it possible? It is possible precisely because the thanking is not an appropriate conclusion inferred from the way things go, but is itself a reaction to, and assessment of, the way things go. The Christian thanks God whatever happens, in the sense that nothing can render loving God pointless. The way things go is contingent, but the possibility of thanking God in all things, a possibility St Paul speaks of, is, Kierkegaard says, part of the eternity which God has put in men's hearts. Indeed, the ability to thank God, to love Him, is only given when man has died to the objective world-historical view of things. The God-given ability to give thanks in all things *is* the goodness of God. This will never be recognized as long as we think that the difficulty facing us is to account for the goodness of God in face of the evil in the world. The goodness of God is a given mode of response to the good and the evil in the world: it is the response of *agape*.

This in no way dispenses with what has been called the problem of evil. On the contrary, it is placed on a new level of seriousness. Many, recognizing belief in God as a response to the good and the evil in life, will call the response itself evil. That cannot be denied. A value judgment is made which condemns the Christian attitude. It is not the business of philosophy to resolve the disagreement – whatever that might mean – but it is the business of philosophy to elucidate its nature. But that is not something we can embark on in this paper.

But what of Professor Flew and Professor Hick's insistence that the love of God must make a difference to the course of men's lives? They are right, of course, in thinking that it must make *some* difference, but they are wrong in the kind of difference they think it ought to make. The kind of difference the love of God makes is no more and no less than the difference involved in dying to what Kierkegaard calls the objective world-historical view of things, and attaining what he calls subjectivity. Christianity is not a religion of consolation and compensation. It is a religion, the God of which, Simone Weil tells us, has only one gift to offer: the gift of grace.

I hope I have been able to give some indication of Kierkegaard's use of the term 'subjectivity'. In some ways it is a dangerous term to use, since we may think he means that whatever an individual says is true *is* true, or that whatever the majority says is true. Nothing could distort Kierkegaard's views more. In his work *Either/Or*[5] and in many of his works, he has nothing but disdain for the lover of the moment, the sensuous man, or for the crowd, the popular vote. But those who think that Kierkegaard's use of 'subjectivity' is akin to any of this must be ignoring the contexts in which he uses the expression. They bring to his work their own acquaintance with the use of the expression and assume, wrongly, that his use of the expression must be the same.

Kierkegaard's use of 'subjectivity' in relation to belief in God does not mean that there are no criteria of truth and falsity, right and wrong, depth and shallowness, involved, since indeed there are. It must be admitted, however, that some of his works do encourage one to think otherwise. I have in mind Kierkegaard's study of the demand Abraham felt God had made on him to sacrifice Isaac, called *Fear and Trembling*.[6] There, Kierkegaard speaks as if one can understand God's commands simply by saying that God had commanded them. One could say 'God commands *x*' where '*x*' could be given any value whatever. Kierkegaard speaks sometimes as if God could ask my neighbour to sacrifice his son, and that in doing so He would be asking him to do *the same* deed as He asked Abraham to perform. I think this is logically absurd. What Abraham was asked to do can only be understood in terms of the context in which the request was made: the religious Jewish family, the status of the first-born, Abraham's status in the tribe, and, of course, the institution of child sacrifice. It is logically impossible for my neighbour to repeat Abraham's action. Even if he discovered the exact route Abraham took to Mount Moriah, even if he discovered the altar, bound his son on it, and raised the knife, he would not be doing what Abraham did. It is no more possible to fulfil the same deed as Abraham attempted than it is to act on the exhortation by the *Daily Express* at the accession of the present Queen to the

throne, and make this another Elizabethan age. 'God
commands', then, does not transcend all communal
contexts. On the contrary, it could only have meaning
in such contexts. An atrocity would not cease to be an
atrocity if one put 'God commands' in front of it. There
are times, therefore, when Kierkegaard's speculations
do make one feel that a greater emphasis on criteria of
divinity which are not the product of individual affirmation would have avoided certain extremities. Many
Christians may feel uneasy to find Kierkegaard asking
whether there can be a teleological suspension of the
ethical, and suggesting that the ethical, what one con-
ceives to be one's duty, could be precisely the opposition
to God's commands.

The misgivings which I have voiced about certain
parts of *Fear and Trembling*, however, are not characteristic of the general character of Kierkegaard's remarks.
In *Either/Or*, in *Purity of Heart*,[7] in the *Postscript*, in
Works of Love,[8] and in other writings, the commands of
God are internally related to the nature of God. There
are certain things which would be nonsensical to place
after 'God commands'. 'God commands the slaughter
of the innocent' is nonsense. God's nature is the grammar of God's will, and Kierkegaard never tires of saying
that God's nature is love. To possess this love is to know
God, to have eternal life, to become subjective.

So, you see, the subjectivity Kierkegaard is talking
about is nothing other than walking with God. And
certainly Kierkegaard is the last to say that it follows
from the fact that a man *says* that he is walking with
God, that he *is* walking with God. Kierkegaard is far
too aware of the snares which beset the Christian's path
to embrace such an optimistic conclusion. In *Purity of*

Heart, Kierkegaard discusses the barriers to willing one thing, willing the Good: attempting to will the good for the sake of a reward, attempting to will the good out of fear of punishment, the egocentric service of the good – that is, being prepared to serve the good only as long as one is prominent as the vehicle of the good – and, finally, willing the good to a certain degree – that is, attempting to subordinate goodness to the dictates of convenience. In *Either/Or,* Kierkegaard discusses the elaborate and complex contortions of the sensuous man in his efforts to convince himself that he possesses the eternal. So Kierkegaard is well aware that the world-historical perspective keeps breaking in on the subjectivity which the Christian struggles to attain. That being so, how can Kierkegaard be accused of an emotional individualism? Is it not clear that Kierkegaard is fully aware of the possibilities of pride, temptation, and self-deception in the realms of faith? So there are criteria of truth and falsity, right and wrong, depth and shallowness, within what Kierkegaard calls 'subjectivity'. But these criteria belong to the realm of faith itself. The love of God is not based on the facts, but is itself the measure by which the Christian assesses the facts. Is not this as it should be from a Christian point of view? Would it not be odd if the Creator were assessed in the light of his creation, rather than the creation being seen in the light of the Creator's nature? Surely this is a desirable orthodoxy in Kierkegaard: God is not to be judged by the world, but the world is to be judged by God.

In discussing the barriers which constantly come between a man and his worship of God, Kierkegaard is emphasizing how great a gulf separates the barriers and the worship. All the barriers belong to the sphere of the world-historical, while worship belongs to the sphere of subjectivity. Having emphasized these differences, Kierkegaard asks us to consider how incredible it is to find people not only glossing over these differences, but actually saying that one could become subjective via the world-historical. To Kierkegaard this is an absurd spectacle: it consists in the attempt to prove the divine by reference to worldliness. He calls it in the *Postscript* the attempt at infinite approximation. The idea seems to be that by gathering sufficient evidence, by amassing sufficient facts, one will somehow make the transition from the world-historical to subjectivity. But the hope is an illusion, for, as we have seen, the required transition is not a matter of degree, but of kind. It is a transition from a quantitative to a qualitative assessment. How could one win assent to qualitative distinctions by a parade of quantitative considerations? Consider the barriers to loving God and the Good which Kierkegaard speaks of. Suppose what appeals to a man is the reward offered. How can a multiplying of such rewards change the nature of his regard? Or suppose that a man conforms to the will of God out of fear of punishment. How can a multiplying of such punishments change the nature of his conformity? The impossibility of a transition from non-moral facts to moral conclusions, or of a transition from the ways of the world to the divine, is something which needs to be recognized in contemporary moral philosophy. Once again, in the revival of ethical naturalism, we see the desire to prove to a man why he should be good. But this desire is based on a deep misunderstanding. Neither divinity nor decency admit of an external proof. They speak an unequivocal language which, demanding to be heard and obeyed, offers no external guarantees, no train of compensations.

Perhaps I can illustrate this further, before ending, by showing how Kierkegaard's reflections help us to understand the Christian notions of eternal life and victory.

Kierkegaard wants to say, in his *Works of Love*,[9] that the Christian believes all things in love and is yet never deceived. From the point of view of the world-historical this is rubbish, for surely the likeliest way of being deceived is by believing all things. If one wishes to avoid being deceived, then instead of believing everything, one must carefully sift the facts. One must see which things, among the many we are asked to believe, we have good grounds for believing. We must be discriminating in giving our assent to beliefs. Clearly, then, if love believes all things, it cannot avoid being deceived.

Now, in one sense, Kierkegaard does not deny any of this. He does not deny that the man who responds in love will be deceived in many ways: that promises made to him will not be kept, that solemn vows to him will be broken, that money owed to him will not be returned, that confidences imparted by him will be betrayed, and so on. Kierkegaard is not denying any of these facts. But for him all these facts remain on a level of quantitative assessment: they are assessments of how the world is likely to treat the lover. Kierkegaard is more interested in another question: how is the lover treating love?

It may be that in face of the setbacks I have mentioned, a person gives up exercising love. In that case, Kierkegaard wants to say, he is more of a loser than his would-be beneficiary. It is possible, Kierkegaard says, for such a man to be led astray by a mistaken analogy. A man who has been a benefactor may become disillusioned at the lack of thanks he receives for his financial gifts. He decides to give no more. In that case, Kierkegaard says, he is richer, since the money he would have given away is now in his pocket. But it is not so with love. You cannot keep love intact, but unused, in your pocket. The adjective 'rich' can apply to a man who does not give his money away, but the adjective 'loving' cannot apply to a man who has ceased to love. As Kierkegaard points out, the very language he uses mocks him, for he says, 'I have ceased to be loving'. So although the man who ceases to receive love loses, so does the man who ceases to give love. He is the greater loser. But that truth admits of no external proof.

But what of God's rewards for the lover? Does not God remember those who abide in love? Yes, Kierkegaard tells us, He does, but His remembering is their loving: to abide in love is love's reward. If this is not understood, Christianity is brought down to the level of the world-historical. Someone might argue that God forgives one's sins only if one forgives the sins committed against one, and that this is why one should forgive wrongs against one. But would this be forgiving? Would it not be a policy of prudence? Would not the person concerned refrain from forgiving if he thought God would not forgive him? This mistaken reasoning must be replaced, Kierkegaard says, by the true Christian view, which is that there is no gap between our forgiveness of other people and God's forgiveness of us. If we have no forgiveness in our hearts, how can we say that we believe in the existence of forgiveness, when, as Kierkegaard says, our own lives show that we do not.

But if we forgive others, then we have the spirit of God in us, and this is our forgiveness. He who loves, Kierkegaard says, is not forgotten. There is one who remembers him – love or God remembers him. He remembers him by abiding in him. It is in this way only, Kierkegaard concludes, that the lover gets what he gives. To abide in love is to possess the victory, and to possess eternal life. The value of loving does not depend on the response. The response is contingent, but the love is eternal; eternal in the sense that its value does not depend on the response.[10]

Contrast this with the arguments of those who want some kind of proof of the worth of love. Consider, for example, Mill's treatment of martyrdom. Mill cannot deny that some people voluntarily sacrifice their own happiness. But, he asks, what is it that these people have sacrificed their happiness for? The answer he gives is that they have done so for the sake of the happiness of others. Mill is quite prepared to say that the self-sacrifice is noble, but he goes on to say that, 'after all, this self-sacrifice must be for some end; it is not its own end. . . . I ask, would the sacrifice be made if the hero or martyr did not believe that it would earn for others immunity from similar sacrifices?'[11]

For Mill, the worthwhileness of the sacrifice depends on the outcome, on how things turn out. This is very clearly stated as follows: 'The utilitarian morality does recognize in human beings the power of sacrificing their own greatest good for the good of others. It only refuses to admit that the sacrifice is itself a good. A sacrifice which does not increase, or tend to increase, the sum total of happiness, it considers as wasted.'[12] For Kierkegaard, this is tantamount to saying that the worthwhileness of sacrifice is dependent on the world-historical. Contrast Mill's treatment of martyrdom with Kierkegaard's remarks on the Crucifixion of Jesus. As far as the world-historical view is concerned,

> nothing in the world has ever been so completely lost as was Christianity at the time that Christ was crucified . . . never in the world had anyone accomplished so little by the sacrifice of a consecrated life as did Jesus Christ. And yet in this same instant, eternally understood, He had accomplished all. . . . Was it not said by many intelligent men and women, 'The result shows that He had been hunting after phantasies; He should have married. In this way He would now have been a distinguished teacher in Israel.'
>
> And yet, eternally understood, the crucified one had in the same moment accomplished all! But the view of the moment and the view of eternity over the same matter have never stood in such atrocious opposition. It can never be repeated. This could happen only to Him. Yet eternally understood, He had in the same moment accomplished all, and on that account said, with eternity's wisdom, 'It is finished.'[13]

So one has a clash between the world-historical view of Jesus's death, and his death viewed subjectively, from the point of view of the eternal, from the perspective of the love of God – all these are synonymous for Kierkegaard. The martyr dies for the love of God or the love of the Good. Even if he dies for a cause, he may not die for the success of the cause – he may die for it whether it is successful or not. He dies for something worth dying for, and that does not depend on the outcome, on how things go. There is a collection of last letters written by various people before they were executed by the Gestapo. The collection has been given the title *Dying We Live*.[14] I am sure that title was given because the letters show that for these people a life of compromise with the Gestapo would have been a form of moral and spiritual death, while death for the sake of what they believed is a form of life. That is an absolute unconditional judgment of value which does not depend on the outcome. These people, like Socrates, were able to say that they would only be ashamed if their death was the result of forsaking the Good. They knew in Germany, as he knew in Athens, that anything might happen to them, but with Socrates they could say, without contradiction, 'All will be well.'[15]

So it is with the Christian, Kierkegaard says. His faith is an absolute in terms of which he meets and assesses the way things go. It is not itself the product of the way things go. Not so the Christians Professor John Hick talks about in his recent inaugural lecture called 'Theology's Central Problem'.[16] For them, faith is faith that things will turn out well in the end; it is a world-historical faith on this view, the conviction that the world is not treating one well should not lead to pessimism, since there is good reason to suppose that one is going to be treated well later. The following quotation from Hick deserves to be treated as a classic statement of world-historical religion:

> . . . in contrast to the tragic character of life as seen by humanism, transcendent theism, in its Jewish and Christian forms, affirms that the divine Mind which

religious faith has seen at work in various revelatory situations is wholly good. It follows from this that the hard travail of human life, as it has been for so many people, is neither pointless nor wasted. For it falls within a purpose which, being divine, is assured of ultimate fulfilment, and being good cherishes the welfare of each individual human being. This present life thus constitutes a chapter in a story which is going eventually to have a happy ending.[17]

Kierkegaard will have none of this. Whatever Christianity is about, it is not about happy endings! Rather, it is about people who strive to be rooted and grounded in the love of God. If the world deals harshly with them, their lives are not, as Hick seems to think, pointless or wasted. On the contrary, if they have possessed the Spirit of God, which, for Kierkegaard, is the Spirit of Love, despite their tribulations, they have accomplished all.

A final note in ending which is rather ironic. What does Kierkegaard have to say about the status of papers such as this one? He points out that it is very easy for his reflections to become themes for lectures in the future. When this happens, the character of the reflections change. They cease to be truths to be expressed in living, and become interesting facts which the professional lecture-goer files away with all his other innumerable interesting facts. The very protest against the world-historical can itself become part of the world-historical – an objective thesis which is recorded but not acted upon. A man can proclaim such theses without believing them. Kierkegaard is savage in his attacks on what he calls 'becoming a town-crier of the eternal'.

In so far as Kierkegaard is condemning the gulf between proclamation and practice, few would disagree with him. But what does that mean for the present paper which claims, at least, to be a philosophical treatment of the theme of subjectivity and truth in Kierkegaard? The implication of what Kierkegaard is saying may be that it is impossible to make a philosophical observation about faith without faith, that one cannot observe that in the realm of faith, truth is subjectivity in Kierkegaard's sense, without becoming subjective oneself, without embracing the truth. If that is an implication of what Kierkegaard is saying, then to this extent what he says is false. But Kierkegaard may be saying something else – namely, that to make philosophical observations about the relation of truth and subjectivity in the realm of faith is very different from actually attaining this subjectivity or embracing this truth. If this is what Kierkegaard is saying, the present writer is more than ready to agree with him.

References

1. This chapter originated as a lecture given to the Southampton Newman Association in a course of lectures on existentialism.
2. Trans. Swenson, David F., Princeton University Press, 1944.
3. See *ibid.*, 147 f.
4. See 'Theology and Falsification' in *New Essays in Philosophical Theology*, ed. Flew and MacIntyre, S.C.M. Press, 1955.
5. Trans Lowrie, Walter, 2 vols., O.U.P., 1946.
6. Trans. Payne, Robert, O.U.P., 1939.

7. Trans. Steere, Douglas, Fontana Books, 1961.
8. Trans. Hong, Howard and Edna, Collins, 1962.
9. See *ibid.*, Part Two, chs. I–III.
10. *Cf.* pp. 27–9.
11. *Utilitarianism*, ed. Warnock, Mary, Fontana Series, 1962, 267.
12. *Ibid.*, 268.
13. *Purity of Heart*, 120–1.
14. Ed. Gollwitzer, H., Kuhn, K., and Schneider, R.; trans. Kuhn, Reinhard C., Fontana Books, 1958.
15. Plato, *The Gorgias*, 521 f.
16. Published by the University of Birmingham, 1967.
17. *Ibid.*, 12.

XI God and Ought

Why should I obey God's commands? Many philosophers suggest that I should do so only if I have judged
that *this* command of God's is good or that *all* God's
commands are good. In other words, an acceptance of
God's commands must depend on my moral judgment.
I want to deny this. I am not denying that one can
understand certain moralities without understanding
religion or that God is sometimes the object of moral
judgment. What I am denying is that the relation
between God and what I ought to do is *necessarily*
parasitic on moral judgment. On the contrary, for
believers, 'good' means 'whatever God wills'.

But is it not obvious that what I have just said cannot
be the case? If 'good' means 'whatever God wills', the
question 'Is what God wills good?' ought to be redundant. Clearly, the question is perfectly meaningful.
Must we not admit, then, that *we* are the ones to decide
whether what God wills is good or not? I do not think
so. Often in the theses of philosophers who argue in this
way, 'good' is a blanket term under which all its com-
plexities and variations slumber unnoticed. I want to
suggest that such arguments cannot account for moral
situations with which we are all perfectly familiar, and
that this failure to account for moral situations applies
equally to religious phenomena. Let us examine these
two shortcomings.

God and Ought

We are often asked in philosophical discussions on morality and religion to distinguish between descriptive statements and evaluative statements. One cannot argue from a descriptive statement about God to the assertion of an obligation to God. Because God is our Father it does not follow that His name should be hallowed. To think otherwise, these philosophers would have us believe, is to confuse the moral and the non-moral; to attempt to derive an 'ought' from an 'is'. But if the Heavenly Father has fared so ill at their hands, would the earthly fathers fare any better? The problem of the nature of the connection between the matter-of-fact status of being a father and the obligations children have to their parents has been treated by A. I. Melden in *Rights and Right Conduct*.[1] Readers will no doubt recognize many of his arguments in the following remarks.

Melden stresses the need to take account of the institution of the family in any explanation of parental rights and the obligations of children to their parents. The only weakness of an otherwise illuminating analysis is what I take to be an over-emphasis on what Melden calls 'the role' of the father. He concentrates too much on what the father does, and too little on who he is – namely, the father of his children. But then Melden speaks sometimes as if this distinction is non-existent; as if what a father is can be explained in terms of what he does. This is especially the case when he talks of the father as forfeiting his rights. The child says to his father, 'You have never been a father to me.' If one fails to play the role of father, one sacrifices one's rights as a father. It must be admitted that there are occasions when we should say that a man is no longer fit to be a

father, and we would not blame the child for disowning
him. ('He drove my mother to her grave.') The trouble
with Melden's way of talking, however, is that it makes
it look as if being a father is a role that *anyone* can play.
He points out, for instance, that the child may come to
regard someone other than his natural father as his
'father'. But there is a difference between a natural
father and a 'father' nevertheless. It is the ignoring of
the connection between fatherhood and nature which
constitutes an important gap in Melden's account. So
many problems concerning the child-parent relationship cannot be understood unless this connection is
recognized. So many of the obligations I have to my
father do not depend on whether he has done things for
me or even on whether he loves me. It is certainly not a
case of tit-for-tat. ('If my father hits me, why shouldn't I
hit him back?') I do not want to deny that imperfec-
tions in the father may lead to his being rejected by the
child. On the other hand, many people would say that
the rejection of the father is an imperfection in the
child; that the child who loves his father only as long as
he is a good father has an imperfect love of his father.
('You should not leave your father destitute in his old
age.' – 'But he never went out of his way to help me.' –
'That doesn't matter.' – 'He never tried to understand
me.' – 'That's not the point.' – 'What is the point
then?' – 'That he is your father.')

'Because he *is* your father': what does this mean?
Surely it refers to the fact that this is the man who begat
you; this is the man to whom you owe your existence.
There is only *one* such man. The sadness of those who
never knew their fathers cannot normally be explained
in terms of what the father has done. Neither can the

restless desire to find a lost father one has never known be explained in this way. These sentiments together with the situations discussed above cannot be understood unless one takes into account, not simply what the father does for his children, but who the father is – namely, the man to whom the children owe their existence.[2] (Is not this the root of the analogy with 'God the Father' – one to whom I owe my existence?)

No doubt I shall be accused by some philosophers of having moved my argument from descriptive to evaluative statements. Evaluative statements are said to depend on my preferences or pro-attitudes. But one cannot understand my obligations to my father in terms of my decision that to obey my father is good. When did I *decide* that I have obligations to my father? Surely, the most natural explanation of my considerate conduct is, 'Because he is my father.' Melden is correct when he says that my father's rights and my obligations to him cannot be understood in isolation from the institution of the family in which these rights and obligations flourish. The distinction between descriptive and evaluative statements in this context is confused and misleading. Outside the institution of the family the fact that this is the man who begat me would not have the moral significance that it has within the family. As Melden points out, the embryological facts about a male parent do not yield the concept 'father' at all. We appreciate the force of a reminder of our obligations when someone says, 'Remember, he is your father.' He does not have to add, 'And you ought to give special consideration to your father', since to understand what is meant by calling someone your father is to understand that one has certain obligations towards him.

It seems, then, that the status of being a father entails certain rights which the children of the father have obligations to satisfy. It is possible to argue from 'He is my father' to 'I ought not to leave him destitute', for example, since the understanding of the latter statement is involved in the understanding of the former. But here the dissenting philosophers could ask, If 'He is my father' means 'I ought to give him special consideration', why is it that I can come to a moral decision on a given occasion not to satisfy my father's rights? But the fact that I decide sometimes not to satisfy my father's rights does not imply that my father only has rights when I decide to satisfy them! Melden exposes the confusion between actions which meet obligations and obligatory actions. I can meet my obligations to my father in a variety of ways. Melden calls these actions 'obligation-meeting' actions. But obligation-meeting actions are not always obligatory. Rights compete for satisfaction. Sometimes I decide that I ought not to give moral satisfaction to my father's rights. If obligation-meeting actions were always obligatory, Melden points out, many familiar moral situations would be distorted or unintelligible. For example, it would be moral depravity to waive one's rights, whereas in fact we often praise people for doing so. Again, moral perplexity over competing rights would not be a practical problem, but a logical absurdity. The question, 'What ought I to do?' does not make the right any less a right, for what one is questioning is not the right, but whether the right is a sufficient reason for action favourable to it in a given situation. The fact that we must decide sometimes what our duty is does not imply that there are no competing rights; it is these rights which make the decision

God and Ought

difficult. Otherwise, what is moral tragedy, where, whatever one does, one is going to hurt someone?

Although Melden seems to contrast his account of moral rights with a religious account of morality, I see no reason why the lesson he teaches in moral philosophy cannot be applied to the philosophy of religion.

To understand what it means to call someone a father is to understand why his children act towards him in certain distinctive ways. To understand what it means to believe in God is to understand why God must be obeyed. Certain actions can only be understood in the light of the child-parent relationship. For example, the fact that I do not hit a man who has hit me is given new significance if I tell you that the man who hit me is my father. Other actions cannot be understood unless one understands that they are responses to God's will – as, for example, the sacrifice of financial betterment in the vocation to the ministry. As in morality, in religion, too, there are reminders of duty in face of laxity: 'Remember the Lord your God.' The prophets said this time and time again to the Children of Israel. There was no need for them to add, 'You ought to obey God.' They *knew* that because they knew *Him*.

But what of the so-called trump card in the argument? If 'good' means 'the commands of God', the question, 'Is the will of God good?' ought to be redundant. But why should the question be redundant? God's will does not cease to mean what it does simply because it is questioned. We saw that moral rights compete for satisfaction, but here the competition is not between rights *within* the same moral community, but between the claims of morality and religion as such. The believer who is not troubled by doubts and to

228

whom life has been kind, does not ask, 'Is what God wills good?' When the question is asked, morality has invaded the realm of religion and the fight is on. The struggle begins simply because the will of God is questioned. It is important to notice, however, that the fight is not confined to one camp. If belief has doubts, so has unbelief: if morality invades religion, religion invades morality. For example, the believer may begin to doubt the goodness of God because of the death of a loved one. On the other hand, the unbeliever may, through the moral experience of his own inadequacy as a person, begin to wonder whether there is something important after all in the idea of divine forgiveness and salvation. The fact that the will of God is questioned does not destroy the internal connection between the will of God and what one ought to do, since when someone is torn between morality and religion what decides the issue is to be found not, as many philosophers think, in an independent moral judgment,[3] but in the nature of the decision – that is, in the relevant moral or religious considerations which win the day.

The religious concept of duty cannot be understood if it is treated as a moral concept. When the believer talks of doing his duty, what he refers to is doing the will of God. In making a decision, what is important for the believer is that it should be in accordance with the will of God. To a Christian, to do one's duty *is* to do the will of God. There is indeed no difficulty in envisaging the 'ethical' as the obstacle to 'duty' in this context. For example, a man may, because of what he takes to be his moral obligations towards his family, refuse to give up his job in response to what he believes is God's call to enter the ministry. The Christian would then say with

Kierkegaard, 'Here there can be no question of ethics in the sense of morality. . . . Ordinarily speaking, a temptation is something which tries to stop a man from doing his duty, but in this case it is ethics itself which tries to prevent him from doing God's will. But what then is duty? Duty is quite simply the expression of the will of God.'[4]

At this point I must warn the reader that despite my remarks hitherto, I am not arguing for a sharp separation between religious discourse and moral discourse. I cannot accept the account offered by some theologians which makes religion appear to be a technical language, cut off, alien and foreign to the language spoken by everyone else in the community. This picture is false and misleading. It cannot account even for religious phenomena, such as the traffic between unbelief and belief. But more important is the fact that it fails to see the importance of calling religion a language or a way of life. Such accounts make religion look like a technique. But a technique in itself could never be a language or a way of life. Religious doctrines, worship, ritual, etc., would not have the importance they do were they not connected with practices other than those which are specifically religious. When a man prays to God for forgiveness, for example, his prayer would be worthless did it not arise from problems in his relationship with other people. These problems can be appreciated by the religious and the non-religious alike. Because of such connections between religious and non-religious activity, it is possible to convey the meaning of religious language to someone unfamiliar with it, even if all one achieves is to stop him from talking nonsense. But one hopes for more than that. By the use of analogies, contrasts, and comparisons with which we can journey so far, but must then discard in favour of others, one hopes to convey something of the meaning and force of religious language. It is not my purpose here to discuss which analogies can best be employed for this task. What I do want to stress is that, despite the existence of connections between religious and non-religious discourse, the criteria of sense and nonsense in the former are to be found *within* religion. It is this religious meaning which the analogies, contrasts, and comparisons try to explain. Just as Melden insists on the basic role to be played by the institution of the family in an explanation of the moral concepts he is dealing with, so I am insisting on a reference to the institution of religion whenever one wants to understand what religious people are saying.

One can be faced with conflicting obligations. Some of these may be obligations to God. Unlike morality, which recognizes that sometimes it is not wrong to decide against one's obligations to one's father, religion recognizes no circumstances in which one is justified in deciding against one's obligations to God. This is because in rejecting God's will one is not rejecting *one* claim among many within an institution such as the family; one is rejecting the foundation of an institution. To reject God's claim is not to reject one of many competing claims in a way of life; it is to reject a way of life as such.

Many philosophers think that moral judgment is necessarily prior to religious assent. Nothing could be further from the truth, for, as Camus says, 'When man submits God to moral judgment, he kills Him in his own heart.'

God and Ought

References

1. Blackwell, 1959.
2. The distortions which result from ignoring this aspect of fatherhood were pointed out to me in discussion by Mr Rush Rhees.
3. What would this *independent* judgment be?
4. *Fear and Trembling*, O.U.P., 1939, 84–5.

XII On The Christian Concept of Love

This chapter is selective, and to that extent, arbitrary. There are many concepts of love (despite the Freudian view) and I do not touch on most of them. There is the love involved in lust, romantic love, the love of average respectable marriages, love of friendship, love of beauty, love of God, and so on. I make no attempt to prove the reality of these ideas of love. I take that for granted. What I want to do is to set out certain problems which arise from *one* idea of love – namely, that found in the Christian commandment to love our fellow men. Certain interpretations of this idea are open to serious moral objections. There is one interpretation of the commandment which avoids these objections, but even this has little, if anything, to say about problems which arise from the nature of human love in certain contexts.

It would be a misunderstanding to look for *the* answer to the problems which I mention in this chapter, since people's answers will be as different as their loves.

Can I be commanded to love? Can I have a duty to love? Kant seemed to think that acting from a sense of duty is acting from the highest motive. But does it make sense to say that I can love a woman out of a sense of duty? Is not this the same as saying that I do not love her at all? True, we often have occasion to point out a husband's obligations to his wife, the parents' obligations to their children, the friend's obligations to his friend. But the occasions on which these reminders are given are those where the relationships referred to have broken down in some way or other: 'You have a duty to your wife. You can't leave her.' – 'Yes, I see that. But I can't love her.'

It is one thing to say that these relationships entail obligations, but quite another thing to say that a sense of duty can be the motive for the love which in ideal cases makes these relationships what they are. Again, duties arise and can be met within these relationships ('No. I'd better not stay. I've promised to take my wife out tonight'), but this is not to say that the relationship can be participated in out of a sense of duty.

In what sense, then, do Christians say that we are commanded to love our fellow men? How can we regard love as a duty? Clearly, I am not called upon to love all women as I love my wife, to love all children as I love my own, to love everyone as I love my friends. But if not, what am I called upon to do when told to love my fellow men?

One cannot understand the Christian love of others unless one understands its connection with love of God. The Christian concept of love is very different from the love found in the relationships we have mentioned, where the love depends on the particularity of the relationship. What does this particularity refer to? Consider marriage: 'Wilt thou have *this* woman . . .?' Am I saying that there is only one girl for you in the world? No! It is not that *this* woman *is* different from all others, but that she *becomes* different from all others in becoming *your wife*. Similarly, my friends are different from other people because they are my friends. But according to Christian teaching, I must love all men because *all men are the same*. They are children of God. But what kind of love is this? '. . . "Thou shalt love." It consists first and foremost in the fact that you must not love in such a way that the loss of the beloved would reveal the fact that you were desperate, that is, that you simply must not love despairingly.'[1]

When the person I love is *this* person rather than another, the death of the beloved is the worst that can happen. This is not so in Christian love of others, since they are loved, not because of their being *these* persons rather than others, but simply because of their *being*. 'The neighbour is your equal. The neighbour is not your beloved for whom you have a passionate partiality. . . . The neighbour is every man. . . . He is your neighbour through equality with you before God. . . .'[2] And again, 'Belief in the existence of other human beings as such is *love*.'[3]

Christian love of fellow men seems to have little in common with the love that exists between husband and wife, parents and children, friend and friend. In many outstanding examples of Christian love – say, St Peter Claver or St Vincent de Paul – charity is shown to those whom the charitable person did not know.

What conclusions can be drawn from these differences between the way the concept of love is used in the Christian commandment and the way it is used elsewhere? What I want to do now is to show how certain possible, if not necessary, implications of the Christian concept of love are open to moral and religious objections, and at the same time try to point to an alternative interpretation of the concept which is free from such censure.

Christianity seeks that which is essential in all men. There are inessential things, but in the last analysis, these can be ignored. But what is this essential thing which all men have in common? Their identity as children of God.

> The difference is the confusion of the temporal existence which marks every man differently, but the neighbour is the mark of the eternal – on every man. Take a number of sheets of paper, write something different on each of them so that they do not resemble each other, but then take again each individual sheet, do not be confused by the different inscriptions, hold it up to the light, and then you can see a common mark in them all. And so the neighbour is the common mark, but you see it only by the light of the eternal, when it shines through the differences.[4]

But what is the mark of the eternal? That is the difficult problem. Christians hold that 'the eternal' has been captured in certain specific propositions about God – for example, that God became incarnate in Jesus of Nazareth. It follows, according to them, that what is of eternal importance is that they should try to get all men to give assent to this special revelation of God. As a matter of fact, this conclusion does not follow at all. Even if you believe that you have eternal truth, it does not follow that you ought to proselytize. One may say that something is the eternal truth, but at the same time stress the importance of each man's coming to it for himself. Many Christians seem to think that men

have a duty to follow *this* way of life rather than another.
This is difficult to understand from a moral point of
view. Certainly, we often condemn those who hold
moral opinions which are different from our own. We
say they are wrong in holding such views. But when the
views and actions in question are tied up with a culture
different from our own, the position is altered. If I hear
that one of my neighbours has killed another neighbour's child, given that he is sane, my condemnation is
immediate. (There are exceptions. See Faulkner's
Requiem for a Nun.) But if I hear that some remote tribe
practises child sacrifice, what then? I do not know what
sacrifice means for the tribe in question. What would it
mean to say I condemned it when the 'it' refers to
something I know nothing about? If I did condemn it I
would be condemning murder. But murder is not child
sacrifice. 'The ethical expression of Abraham's action is
that he wished to murder Isaac: the religious expression
is that he wished to sacrifice him.'[5]

My moral opinions are bound up with the way of life
I lead. Various influences have helped to shape my
morality. This does not mean that when I make moral
judgments I say anything about the way of life I lead or
that the meaning of the moral judgments can be
expressed in terms of the influences which, in part,
account for them. For example, a person brought up in
the Welsh Nonconformist tradition is likely to have
strong views on what activities should be allowed on a
Sunday – views either in sympathy with or in reaction
against the tradition. When he makes his moral judgment on this matter, however, he is not saying anything
about the tradition, but about what activities ought to
be allowed on a Sunday. I must, on the other hand,

understand the significance of actions before I can judge them.[6] My understanding is not limited by one tradition, I understand something of the other traditions within the same culture, however vague my grasp of them may be. For example, in belonging to one tradition of Christian worship one usually has some idea of the other traditions as well. When we consider different cultures, however, the position is altered radically. What should Buddhists do on Sunday? When I do not understand ways of life and worship different from my own, I had better refrain from judging.

But do Christians need to understand? Sometimes they speak as if even within the same culture there were only one morality; as if all one has to determine is whether what one judges is the same as or different from what one believes. If what one judges is the same, it is true; if different, it is false. The question is whether Christianity allows a *serious* consideration of competing moralities and religions. Must it not say that these are part of the inessential in man, the confusing inscriptions which hide from us the common mark in all men – their identity as children of God? But can one speak of competing moralities as incidental and peripheral? Are they not rooted and grounded in the actual ways of life that men pursue?

The first point to be made is just that there are different moralities, opposing sets of rules of human behaviour. This is because there are different ways of life, different 'movements', each with its own rules of procedure for its members. Such rules, it may be noted, need not have been formulated; but the more important point is that formulated or unformulated,

they are not to be regarded as preceptual or man-
datory . . . the moral question is of how people do
behave and not of their 'obeying the moral law';
obedience, or the treating of something as an authority, is just one particular way of behaving, the moral
characterization of which has still to be given. The
phrase 'how people do behave' may be misleading
here. It is not a question of taking any type of activity
in isolation; we do not have a morality until we have
a way of life, a number of ways of behaving that hang
together, that constitute a system – and it is in the
conflict of such systems that rules come to be formulated. From this point of view it might be best to say
that a morality *is* a way of life or a movement; and
in that case the person who spoke in the name of
'morality' would be neglecting to specify the movement he represented.[7]

But am I mistaken in thinking that Christianity does
speak in the name of 'morality', *the* way, *the* truth, and *the*
life? These other beliefs and ways of life must consist of
what is inessential. But how far is one justified in ridding
men of the inessential in order that they gain the essential
truth? How high a price can be put on truth? If you
say that no price is too high, the logic of persecution is
complete. The end justifies the means. To torture or to
kill (the means) is justified by the resultant confession
(the end). On the other hand, you may say that some
prices are too high. Christians say that only free confession is worthwhile. But it is notoriously difficult to
know where to draw the line. Persecutors are obsessed
by the idea that a free confession is just out of reach:
'A little more . . . a little longer . . . and then perhaps

. . .'[8] and so on. Because of the supposition that most men confess belief at the hour of death ('Who is to know what a man says to his God at such a time?') one can never tell whether the end justified the means. Camus notes that Scheler sees Christian neighbour-love and humanitarianism as two sides of the same coin. Such love is an excuse for oppression, and Scheler claims that it is always accompanied by misanthropy. 'Humanity is loved in general in order to avoid loving anybody in particular.'[9]

But as Camus points out, there is another kind of love of humanity. It does not involve elevating 'the essential' above all else. It is the love of humanity of which Ivan Karamazov speaks. Each individual is accepted as he is. The death of *one* child is too high a price for *harmony*. If anything is essential, it is 'the individual good' as opposed to 'the common good', 'eternal truth', etc. As Kant expressed the matter, human beings should be treated '*never merely as means*, but in every case *at the same time as ends in themselves*'.[10]

Is there an interpretation of the Christian concept of love which is not open to the moral objections we have mentioned? I think there is. To show this, it is necessary, of course, to deny that what we have considered hitherto is the Christian concept of love. Think of Kierkegaard's remark concerning the concept, 'The neighbour is every man. . . . He is your neighbour through equality with you before God.' The kind of relationship between believer and unbeliever which we have considered is not a relationship of equality, but of inequality: one had the truth while the other had nothing. The 'truth' is considered to be so important

that any treatment of the unbeliever is justified if it leads
to assent to the truth. For Simone Weil, this is a distortion of the Christian concept of love. The special
revelation is loved more than the neighbour; love of
dogma replaces love of man. It is in this way that
atrocities are committed in the name of love. The kind
of religion one supports depends on whether one loves
dogma or whether one loves man. The way towards
love of God cannot begin with the former.

Simone Weil calls love of man a 'form of the implicit
love of God'. She contrasts this with the moral distinction between justice and charity. Simone Weil considers the account of Thucydides of the ultimatum the
Athenians gave to the people of Melos when they asked
them to join them in their war against Sparta. The men
of Melos invoked justice, 'imploring pity for the anti-
quity of their town'. The Athenians brush aside this
reference to justice, saying:

'Let us treat rather of what is possible. . . . You know
it as well as we do; the human spirit is so constituted
that what is just is only examined if there is equal
necessity on both sides. But if one is strong and the
other weak, that which is possible is imposed by the
first and accepted by the second.'

The men of Melos said that in the case of a battle
they would have the gods with them on account of
the justice of their cause. The Athenians replied that
they saw no reason to suppose so:

'As touching the gods we have the belief, and as
touching men the certainty, that always by a necessity of nature, each one commands wherever he has
the power. We did not establish this law, we are not

the first to apply it; we found it already established, we abide by it as something likely to endure for ever; and that is why we apply it. We know quite well that you also, like all the others, once you reached the same degree of power, would act in the same way.'[11]

According to Simone Weil, most people have gone a step further than the Athenians, who at least recognized that they were brushing aside considerations of justice in accepting as justice what one can be reasonably expected to do or what one can reasonably expect to receive in a given situation. If one's conception of justice varies with the circumstances, then it is likely that whenever one has the power to command, one will do so. When such a concept of justice is found in religion, it tends to be located in the so-called justice of a cause – the cause of a particular religion. No atrocity can be an injustice if it can be shown to further the cause. Simone Weil accuses the Hebrew religion of this distortion: confusing love of man with love of the cause. 'The religions which represent divinity as commanding wherever it has the power to do so are false. Even though they are monotheistic they are idolatrous.'[12]

True religion, for Simone Weil, is the religion which manifests true love. But what is this idea of love? If we hold the relativistic concept of justice, we shall regard charity as a supererogatory act: as something we need not have done. According to Simone Weil, the Christian concept of love does not recognize this distinction. It equates justice and charity. How does this come about?

To answer the above question one must distinguish between two important concepts in Simone Weil's thought: 'attachment' and 'detachment'. 'Attachment' belongs to all relationships of inequality: the strong and the weak, the conqueror and the conquered, employer and employee, and so on. Justice in these relationships is what the strong, for instance, can reasonably be expected to give, and what the weak can reasonably expect to receive. Charity would then be giving more than one is expected to give as an employer, let us say: 'Beyond a certain degree of inequality in the relations of men of unequal strength, the weaker passes into a state of matter and loses his personality. The men of old used to say: "A man loses half his soul the day he becomes a slave."'[13]

On rare occasions, however, we find a person not using his power, but instead, having compassion on the person to whom he stands in a relationship of inequality. Simone Weil calls this 'the supernatural virtue of justice', and says that it 'consists of behaving exactly as though there were equality when one is the stronger in an unequal relationship'.[14] This is where 'detachment' is important. It is the possibility of acting in a way which is not determined by the relative criteria of reasonableness which function in unequal relationships. It is the possibility of detaching oneself from one's special status, and seeing the other as an equal. Simone Weil says that 'He who treats as equals those who are far below him in strength really makes them a gift of the quality of human beings, of which fate had deprived them'.[15] We recall her other remark: 'Belief in the existence of other human beings as such is *love*.'[16]

Compassion is not easy to achieve. It is easy enough to give bread to the starving, money to the needy or clothes to the naked. It is not surprising that a person does these things. 'What is surprising,' as Simone Weil says, 'is that he should be capable of doing so with so different a gesture from that with which we buy an object. Alms-giving when it is not supernatural is like a sort of purchase. It buys the sufferer.'[17]

It is difficult to act from compassion partly because it involves a contemplation of other people as one's equal. This contemplation is akin to another form of the implicit love of God which Simone Weil talks about – namely, the love of the beauty of the world. In some ways, this is easier to understand because it is a more common experience. For example, when ambition threatens to destroy us, and we have come to regard everyone and everything as instruments for our own use, what Simone Weil calls 'The love we feel for the splendour of the heavens, the plains, the sea and the mountains, for the silence of nature' can give us is something which cannot be used – namely, the beauty of the world. One cannot use beauty; one can only contemplate it, since, as Simone Weil says, 'it only gives itself, it never gives anything else'.[18] By this kind of contemplation one's self-centredness is destroyed. One is able 'to see the true centre outside the world'. This contemplation of the beauty of the world – cf. Wittgenstein: 'Not *how* the world is, is the mystical, but *that* it is'[19] – has a parallel in the love of one's neighbour. People can be seen not in relation to my needs and uses, but as human beings – not *how* they are (rich, poor, educated, ignorant, useful, useless, etc.), but *that* they are. Simone Weil says that this act of contemplation 'places the Good outside this world, where are all the sources of power'.[20] Her own life illustrates the kind of powers of courage and endurance given to those who possess this love.

It is important to note that Simone Weil did not think it necessary that those who possessed this love should attribute it to God. She did think, however, that such love is religious and the result of divine activity. This was partly due to her insistence that this love could not be achieved by an effort of will; it only comes by contemplation. That is why she calls it a gift; for her, a gift from God. One has a duty to wait on God, but one cannot have a duty to receive. Simone Weil also thought that this form of implicit love of God leads to a more explicit love of God. It is outside my present task to discuss the difficult question of how this is brought about. All I have been concerned to show is that there is one interpretation of the Christian concept of love which is free from the moral objections we have considered hitherto.

Why do I call Simone Weil's treatment of the concept of love an *interpretation* of the Christian concept? I do so because some of the implications of her standpoint are contrary to orthodox Christian teaching. One of the most important implications of her analysis is that it leaves no place of priority for any one religion. The third form of implicit love of God Simone Weil considers is the love of religious practices. She holds the view that the kind of contemplation she has been considering takes place most naturally within the religion of one's own land and culture. 'All religions pronounce the name of God in their particular language.'[21]

A man can call on God best in his own language and idiom. There should be no searching for words in such worship. Simone Weil cannot give assent to the Christian desire and policy to change men's religious allegiances. Can Christianity take other religions seriously?

It is not a case of Christianity being a *better* religion. This would assume the existence of an objective religious norm. But is the norm any more than what we believe in? If any part of the beliefs of other religions is true, it is regarded as *an approximation to Christian truth*. Christians then say that it follows that a love of men involves the desire to bring them from approximate to complete truth. Hence missionaries. It is the identification of complete truth with Christian truth which has inspired religious protests like that of Simone Weil:

> Personally, I should never give as much as a sixpence towards any missionary enterprise. I think that for any man a change of religion is as dangerous a thing as a change of language is for a writer. It may turn out a success, but it may have disastrous consequences. . . .
>
> The various authentic religious traditions are different reflections of the same truth, and perhaps equally precious. But we do not realize this, because each of us lives only one of these traditions and sees the others from the outside.[22]

The claim of any religion to have the whole truth distorts love of man into love of dogma. Simone Weil recognizes the difficulty of comparative religion as a study, since each religion must be understood from the inside. Understanding can only come, if at all, through a sympathetic bond with the religion in question. But, as Simone Weil says: 'This scarcely ever happens, for some have no faith, and the others have faith exclusively in one religion and bestow upon the others the sort of attention we give to strangely shaped shells.'[23] Simone Weil is not, of course, advocating a rejection of allegi-

ance to particular religions. She sees too clearly how
so-called impartiality can lead to a vague and empty
religiosity. What she is saying is that such allegiance
need not lead one to make claims to possess the entire
truth. Sympathetic understanding of other religions is
the necessary condition for retracting such a claim.

On the other hand, *all* religions are not suited for
what Simone Weil calls, 'calling on the name of the
Lord'. We have seen already how love of dogma, and
belief in the infallibility of a cause can lead to a religion
very different from the kind she advocates. Dostoevsky
called such a religion the religion of the devil. His Grand
Inquisitor says to Christ, who has re-visited the earth:

'We are not working with Thee, but with *him* – that
is our mystery. It's long – eight centuries – since we
have been on *his* side and not on Thine. Just eight
centuries ago, we took from him what Thou didst
reject with scorn, that last gift he offered Thee,
showing Thee all the kingdoms of the earth. We took
from him Rome and the sword of Caesar, and proclaimed ourselves sole rulers of the earth, though
hitherto we have not been able to complete our work.
But whose fault is that? Oh, the work is only beginning, but it has begun. It has long to await completion and the earth has yet much to suffer, but we
shall triumph and shall be Caesars, and then we
shall plan the universal happiness of man.'[24]

By what criterion does Simone Weil call such religion
false? How is she able to judge that 'The true God is the
God we think of as almighty, but as not exercising His
power everywhere'?[25] She says that 'Those of the
Athenians who massacred the inhabitants of Melos had

no longer any idea of such a God'.[26] All right, but they
did have an idea of God. How can one prove that this
idea of God is wrong? Simone Weil answers as follows:
'The first proof that they were in the wrong lies in the
fact that, contrary to their assertion, it happens, though
extremely rarely, that a man will forbear out of pure
generosity to command where he has the power to do so.
That which is possible for man is possible also for God.'[27]

In this answer, Simone Weil is profoundly right.
What other proof of the truth of a religion could one
ever ask for or hope to possess?

Before ending, I want to consider another major
difficulty. I said at the outset that even the interpretation of the Christian concept of love which avoids many
moral objections has little to say about problems which
arise from human love in certain contexts. Examples of
these problems must now be considered.

Love found in intimate human relationships often
gives rise to moral perplexity. When such situations
occur, what has Christianity to say? In a moral perplexity the question I ask myself is, 'What ought I to
do?' I have no clear-cut choice between right and
wrong. I have conflicting obligations. No reference to a
categorical law or immovable principles seems to help.
But is not this what Christianity does? Does it not take a
strange view of such problems by ignoring their complexity and by treating them as problems of casuistry?
Is Christianity any more than 'thou shalt' and 'thou
shalt not'?

But of course it is. There is a distinction between the
general will of God and the special will of God. The
general will of God refers to anything it makes sense to

call the will of God. The special will of God is what God wants me to do here and now in this situation. But not only moral principles clash, divine precepts clash too, leaving the believer praying to know the will of God. There is religious perplexity as well as moral perplexity.

But there is a difference. Even when I do not know the will of God for me, I can rule out certain answers because *they could not* be the will of God. The known will of God is 'the given' in terms of which the problem must be solved. If I believe, I must start 'here' and bring all else into relation with 'the here'. In moral perplexity I do not start anywhere in that sense. Certain difficulties arise which call for some kind of an answer. My answer need not conform to any pre-established code, however. The question is, 'What can I do?' (This is not a question about logical possibilities!) 'What can I do and still live with myself as a person?' No one outside the dilemma can answer the question.

What does Christianity say in face of such situations? Simone Weil herself has some strange things to say. She is suspicious of most forms of human attachment. She claims that this attachment can arise from two motives – namely, from a recognition of good in the loved one or from a need for the loved one. Simone Weil holds the view that there is evil involved in love which arises solely from need. She even compares it with drunkenness and avarice: 'that which was at first a search for some desired good is transformed into a need by the mere passage of time'.[28] When this happens between persons, 'When the attachment of one being to another is made up of need and nothing else', then, according to Simone Weil, 'it is a fearful thing. Few things in this world can reach such a degree of ugliness and horror.'[29]

But if we think of examples of human love where the need for the loved one has destroyed the people involved, would we feel happy about talking in this way? Consider Tolstoy's *Anna Karenina* or Hardy's *Jude the Obscure*. We might call what happened to Anna and Vronsky or to Sue and Jude tragic, but surely not ugly or horrible! Simone Weil seems far too concerned with the preservation of the autonomy of the people involved in such relationships. In order to preserve this autonomy she advocates what she calls 'transforming affection into friendship'.[30] 'Do not allow yourself to be imprisoned by any affection. Keep your solitude.'[31] This may have some point where friendship is concerned, but it seems out of place in relationships such as those between husband and wife, lover and loved one, or parents and children. Here, one is often involved through mutual need in precisely the kind of way which Simone Weil deplores. Apart from advocating detachment, she has nothing positive to say about the problems which arise from the nature of such love. We are still faced with such problems as those portrayed by Tolstoy and Hardy.

Consider the situation in *Jude the Obscure*. Sue and Jude are both unhappily married. They love each other and want to live with each other. They regard marriage as sacred, but on the other hand Jude was tricked into marriage, while Sue married out of a 'love of being loved'. Eventually, Sue goes to live with Jude, but her conflict is not resolved; indeed, it is just beginning. She has a choice: she can either stay with Jude or return to the husband she does not love. She knows that if she leaves Jude it will break him, and yet, in the end, this is what she does. We may feel uneasy about her choice.

We might have chosen differently, but then it would have been our problem and not Sue's. In dilemmas such as this, if one asks the person involved who is to decide what he ought to do, the appropriate answer is, 'I am.'

Tolstoy's Anna decides differently. She stays with her lover, though she realizes that the social death to which the relationship has condemned her is slowly destroying her as a person. She ends it all in suicide. What would Christians say about these decisions? That Sue did the will of God, I suppose. But did she have obligations to Jude? What is one to say to Anna? Repent and return to God?

I am not denying that prayer and the kind of contemplation Simone Weil advocates can help in the case of some problems. For example, a marriage may look like breaking up. The husband and wife think at first that parting is the only answer. On the other hand, if the husband and wife pray about their difficulties, they may, through prayer, find a way of going on which preserves some integrity in their relationship. It may not be the life they dreamed of when they started their married life, but it is something, nevertheless, which gives their marriage a meaning. In the very act of praying, and the kind of reflection on one's life this involves, the possibility of a new way through difficulty is seen.

On the other hand, prayer and reflection seem out of place in other situations, such as those described by Tolstoy and Hardy. This is partly because although waiting on God may bring new insight to a perplexity, the insight must be in accordance with the known will of God. Any answer is not permissible. Most Christians, I take it, would say that it cannot be the will of God for Anna to stay with Vronsky or for Sue to remain with

Jude. This is the difficulty. What morality allows to be considered as a serious possibility, religion dismisses. Such dismissal ignores the complexity of such situations. It will not do simply to call these tragedies horrible or ugly. Neither will it do to say, as many Christians tend to, that had it not been for sin these situations would not have occurred. In the novels mentioned, Christians might say, 'But for the sin of adultery the tragedies would not have occurred.' Even so, now that sin *has* occurred, what does Christianity say about obligations created in sinning? Or can there be no obligation as the result of sin?

In any case, sin will not explain all tragedies. In Faulkner's *Pantaloon in Black* the Negro whose young wife dies gets drunk and kills a workmate who had made a habit of tormenting him. The story illustrates what Simone Weil says about such relationships: 'When the degree of necessity is extreme, deprivation leads to death. This is the case when all the vital energy of one being is bound up with another by some attachment.'[32]

What ought he not to have done in order to avoid ending his life in tragedy? The answer, I presume, is: loved his wife so much. But how odd to say, as Simone Weil does, that what such people ought to do is 'to transform affection into friendship', or to say with Kierkegaard, 'you must not love in such a way that the loss of the beloved would reveal the fact that you were desperate . . .'.[33] In the relationships we have considered, how could the death or deprivation of the loved one reveal anything else?

As I said at the outset, there is no one answer to the jungle of problems arising from the Christian concept of love. This chapter simply tries to show that these problems are more complex than we often suppose, and that there are more problems than we care to think, to which God alone has the answers.

References

1. Kierkegaard, *Works of Love*, O.U.P., 1946, 34.
2. *Ibid.*, 50.
3. Weil, Simone, *Gravity and Grace*, Routledge, 1952, 56.
4. *Works of Love.*
5. Kierkegaard, *Fear and Trembling*, O.U.P., 1939, 34.
6. The concept of 'understanding' actions is of central importance for moral philosophy, and requires far more attention than the passing reference I give it above. To pursue the concept, however, would take the argument too far from the track I want to follow.
7. Anderson, John, 'Art and Morality', *Australasian Journal of Psychology and Philosophy*, December 1941, 255–6.
8. I owe this observation on the psychology of persecution to Professor G. P. Henderson.
9. *The Rebel*, Peregrine ed., 24.
10. *Fundamental Principles of the Metaphysic of Ethics*, trans. Abbott, 1949 ed., 52.
11. *Waiting on God*, Fontana, Ed., 98–9.
12. *Ibid.*, 102.
13. *Ibid.*, 100.
14. *Ibid.*
15. *Ibid.*, 101.
16. See p. 235.
17. *Waiting on God*, 104.
18. *Ibid.*, 122.
19. *Tractatus*, 6.44.
20. *Waiting on God*, 105.

On *The Christian Concept of Love*

21. *Ibid.*, 136.
22. *Letter to a Priest*, Routledge, 1953, 10 and 11.
23. *Waiting on God*, 137.
24. *The Brothers Karamazov*, Bk. V, ch. v.
25. *Waiting on God*, 101.
26. *Ibid.*
27. *Ibid.*
28. *Ibid.*, 155.
29. *Ibid.*
30. *Ibid.*; see p. 158.
31. *Gravity and Grace*, 60.
32. *Ibid.*, 155.
33. See p. 235.

XIII Faith and Philosophy

Let us begin by considering a well-known scene from Plato's *Phaedo*. Simmias and Cebes have just completed their objections against Socrates's arguments for the immortality of the soul. Socrates, having summarized their objections, says:

> To sum up then, if this is the truth, any man who is confident in the face of death must be possessed of a foolish confidence, unless he can demonstrate that the soul is completely immortal and imperishable: and failing this, a man on the point of death must always be afraid that his soul may utterly perish in this impending separation from the body.[1]

When those listening hear this conclusion, they become depressed and dejected. They had believed in the arguments Socrates had put forward, but now those arguments seem to have been discredited. But their depression and despondency has a deeper source than this. The discussion of the immortality of the soul is being carried on by a man awaiting execution. His attitude to his own death is bound to be affected by the outcome of the argument. No wonder, then, that the friends of Socrates feel depressed.

Yet everyone finds Socrates's reaction to the objections of Simmias and Cebes to be admirable. He appreciates the effects the objections have had, but asks his friends to review the arguments against him. He urges them not to become misologists – that is, haters of argument. He compares misology with misanthropy. People become victims of misanthropy by placing too much confidence in their fellow-countrymen, thinking them all to be honest and just. When this confidence is shattered, people then go to the other extreme, and say that no man can be trusted. They become completely sceptical about human nature. It is this extreme scepticism that Socrates wants to draw attention to in talking about misanthropy. Similarly, when men argue, think an argument is sound, and then find that they have to revise it, not once, but many times, they come to the conclusion that there is no soundness in any argument: 'there is nothing sound or stable either in things or in arguments, but . . . everything is . . . in constant ebb and flow and never for any length of time remains at rest'.[2] But, Socrates continues, how pitiful a thing it would be if a man, because of his experience in arguing, having to revise his arguments not once, but many times, fails to blame his own lack of ability, and blames argument instead, by so doing missing the opportunity of arriving at the truth. He continues for the rest of his life 'hating and abusing arguments', and thus 'robs himself of the truth and knowledge of realities'.[3]

What, then, does Socrates recommend? ' "First of all, then," he said, "let us beware of admitting into our souls the thought that probably no arguments are sound: we should much rather admit that we ourselves are not yet sound".'[4] Or, in the words of another translator, ' "Very well," he said, "that is the first thing we must guard against; we must not let it enter our minds that there may be no validity in arguments. On the contrary, we should recognize that we ourselves are still intellectual invalids."' Once we have recognized that we are intellectual invalids, the next thing we must do is strive to become sound. Socrates says that those listening to him should strive for the truth for the sake of the rest of their lives, whereas he, Socrates, should do so for the sake of his impending death. If he does not take the objections of Simmias and Cebes seriously, Socrates will not be facing his death philosophically. He says, 'I am afraid that at the present I am not facing it like a philosopher but am merely bent upon victory, like those who are utterly devoid of culture. For they, whenever engaged in any dispute, care nothing for the truth of the matter under discussion, but are eager only to enforce their own point of view upon their hearers.'[5]

We can recall here the great dispute between Plato and the Sophists. The latter denied that there was any difference between truth and falsity. In an argument, they were not concerned with its truth, but simply with its power of persuasion. This is the scepticism Socrates and Plato are fighting against. The Sophists were only concerned with themselves or with their clients. Given the ends they or their clients wished to attain, the only task remaining was to discover the arguments which would secure those ends. Contrast this with Socrates's exhortation to his friends: 'If you will heed my advice, you will care but little about Socrates, but much more about the truth: and if you think there is any truth in what I say, agree with it, but if not, fight me with every possible argument: and beware that I do not in my zeal deceive both myself and you, and then fly away leaving my sting in you like a bee.'[6]

The distinction drawn here between Socrates and the

truth is extremely important. Kierkegaard sees it as constituting the essence of what he calls 'Socratic heroism'. He elaborates on the meaning of this heroism in his book, *Philosophical Fragments*.[7] In that work, Kierkegaard considers the relation between the philosophical teacher and his pupil. Kierkegaard points out that if we say that Socrates made us understand something, the relation between Socrates and the understanding is nevertheless a contingent one; that is, to give an account of what such understanding comes to is not to give an account of Socrates. The teacher is simply the occasion for the pupil's understanding.

> From the standpoint of the Socratic thought [Kierkegaard says], every point of departure in time is *eo ipso* accidental, an occasion, a vanishing moment. The teacher himself is no more than this; and if he offers himself and his instruction on any other basis, he does not give but takes away, and is not even the other's friend, much less his teacher.[8]

What one understands through the instruction is not the teacher, but the philosophical problem one is dealing with. The philosopher must be prepared to go wherever his questions take him. The pursuit of understanding is greater than the human teacher. It may be true, if one has been taught by a good teacher and a forceful one, that the way one came to see a point cannot be separated from the way one was taught to see the point. The making of a point in philosophy may be closely tied up with the way the point was made, and that way may be inextricable from the style of speech or writing which belongs to the person who made the point. Yet, granting this, it is still true to say that philosophy is wider than any teacher or pupil we may refer to, and thus cannot be explained exhaustively by reference to either. Kierkegaard says again of the teacher-pupil relationship:

> As between man and man no higher relationship is possible; the disciple gives occasion for the teacher to understand himself, and the teacher gives occasion for the disciple to understand himself. When the teacher dies he leaves behind him no claim upon the soul of the disciple, just as the disciple can assert no claim that the teacher owes him anything.[9]

Thus, it is a misunderstanding on the part of a teacher to expect the pupil to follow his views. The pupil may follow them, but if he does it must be because he has made those views his own, and not because they are the views of the teacher. Similarly, it would be a misunderstanding on the part of the pupil to think that he should simply reproduce the teacher's views, and expect the teacher to react favourably. If the pupil reached a philosophical understanding of the subject investigated, the teacher could be dispensed with. Indeed, as in the case of Plato, the pupil may become a greater philosopher than his teacher. Kierkegaard says: 'In the Socratic conception the teacher's love would be merely that of a deceiver if he permitted the disciple to rest in the belief that he really owed him anything, instead of fulfilling the function of the teacher to help the learner become sufficient to himself.'[10] This is not to say that one cannot feel gratitude to or for one's teacher. Kierkegaard's points are philosophical, not biographical.

Compare Kierkegaard's last remark about the teacher's being a deceiver if he allows the pupil to think

that he really owes him anything, with Socrates's
remark that he does not want his zeal for the belief in
the immortality of the soul to deceive others or himself.
He does not want others to agree with him for his sake:
think not of Socrates, but think of the truth. If he
allowed them to agree with him for his sake, he would
have made an illegitimate claim upon them. They
would believe for the sake of Socrates on the day of his
execution. And, after his death, would they not still be
subject to the same pressure to believe for the sake of
Socrates; to refuse to believe that Socrates had died
deluded? Socrates would have flown away like a bee,
but left his sting, the poison of delusory beliefs, in his
hearers. Socrates wants to believe and understand the
immortality of the soul philosophically, not self-
assertively. Let us examine the implications of his
remarks for religious beliefs.

We can begin by noting a fact with which few, I
think, would disagree – namely, that we can continue
to hold beliefs nominally when they have long ceased to
mean anything to us. The nominal life of a belief may
exceed its actual life. This is often the case because the
belief in question remains unexamined. When it is
examined, its emptiness for us becomes apparent. The
examination by which this discovery is made may or
may not be philosophical. Sometimes, no explicit
examination need take place: the occasion, opportunity,
or invitation to examine may prove sufficient in itself to
reveal the emptiness of the belief. Tolstoy provides a
good example of what I have in mind:

> S., a clever and truthful man, once told me the story
> of how he ceased to believe. On a hunting expedition,

when he was already twenty-six, he once, at the place where they put up for the night, knelt down in the evening to pray – a habit retained from childhood. His elder brother, who was at the hunt with him, was lying on some hay and watching him. When S. had finished and was settling down for the night, his brother said to him: 'So you still do that?'

They said nothing more to one another. But from that day S. ceased to say his prayers or go to church. And now he has not prayed or received Communion for thirty years. And this not because he knows his brother's convictions and has joined in them, nor because he has decided anything in his own soul, but simply because a word spoken by his brother was like the push of a finger on a wall that was ready to fall by its own weight. The word only showed that where he thought there was faith, in reality there had long been an empty space, and that therefore the utterance of words and the making of signs of the cross and genuflections while praying were quite senseless actions. Becoming conscious of their senselessness he could not continue them.[11]

The fact that a belief is nominal may be revealed in a more explicit way. It may be revealed through philosophical enquiry. When you embark on an intellectual clarification of your beliefs, you may come to the conclusion that in fact they mean little to you.

But these are not the main examples I have in mind. Philosophy may force us to give up our beliefs, not by showing us that our beliefs were merely nominal, but by showing us that our beliefs are confused and misconceived. In the *Phaedo*, for example, such misconceptions

261

are illustrated by the tendency of thinking of the immortality of the soul in terms of survival after death, which Socrates attacks. This might be a belief held with the kind of zeal that Plato refers to: a zeal fostered by the natural desire to see loved ones again, and to make amends for wrongs committed. The zeal of the believer may be such that he will not listen to any philosophical arguments or take part in any philosophical discussion. In that case, to use Socrates's terminology, we might say that the belief is held self-assertively, and not philosophically. There is a certain antagonism to philosophy that can be explained in this way. When religious believers pursue the subject despite prior warnings, and fail, it is suggested that this is not a case of a student failing a subject, but of a subject failing a student! Here, religious zeal may cover a multitude of confusions.

So far, then, it seems that Socrates is suggesting that religious beliefs, such as belief in the immortality of the soul, must be held philosophically and not self-assertively. The belief must stand up to philosophical scrutiny. We must be open to such scrutiny, and not let our zeal and our desires distort reality. However much we want something to be so, that does not make it so. If what we believe in is the product of confusion, we must give it up. Our motto might well be: *Think not of Socrates, think of the truth.*

But will it do to say that someone can only be said to believe in the immortality of the soul if he can give a philosophical account of his belief? I am not thinking now of immortality construed as survival, but of the radically different account of the immortality of the soul which is connected with purification and dying to the world. The man who believes in the immortality of the soul in this sense has no expectations of certain events taking place after his death. His concern is with the life that the soul ought to strive after. Life, for him, is a kind of purificatory rite. Now we can imagine a person striving to live this life, and yet being quite hopeless at giving a philosophical account of the nature of his belief. Is such a person obliged to give a philosophical account of his belief? I cannot see that he is. The philosopher must always beware against equating the account people give of their beliefs with the actual beliefs these people hold. One must remember that the ability to believe is not the same as the ability to give an account of one's belief. To find out what a belief meant to a person, one would have to come to know that person fairly well. It is not sufficient to listen to what he says about his beliefs, since what he says may be radically confused. What one must pay attention to is the role a belief plays in a person's life, the difference it makes to his life. It is in this context that the meaning of the belief is discovered best.

Does the slogan we have adopted, *Think not of Socrates, think of the truth*, apply in the above context? Think of someone whose life shows the kind of love of the Good that Socrates and Kierkegaard would have commended, but who, when asked, gives a naïve philosophical account of what he believes. Is it clear that here we must not think of the person concerned, but only of the truth? It may be that if we were to try to convince him that his account of his belief was wrong, he would not only give up his account, but give up his belief as well. How important is his account if his life bears witness to the depth of his beliefs? Would it not be foolish to disturb what he says? After all, the person concerned may not be studying philosophy. He may not even be interested in philosophical questions. So why should we place such an emphasis on the correctness of his philosophical account of his belief? Deep convictions can be accompanied by confused accounts of belief, since, as far as I can see, there is no contradiction in saying that someone is both a spiritual giant and an intellectual invalid. So it would be wrong in these circumstances to ignore the people concerned, and simply stress the necessity for philosophical clarity and correctness. Nothing illustrates this better than the folly of newly ordained priests and ministers who see their task as that of making their people intellectually respectable, or the foolishness of those with a little philosophy who set about correcting the allegedly absurd beliefs of their elders.

What has to be remembered, however, is that so far we have considered the motto, *Think not of Socrates, think of the truth,* from the point of view of a believer in the immortality of the soul. Socrates, on the other hand, was talking about philosophical enquiry when he advocated allegiance to the truth. Let us now consider the matter from that starting-point.

Is it true, in the above context, that belief in the immortality of the soul is one thing, and that philosophical enquiry is another? One cannot, without the risk of misunderstanding, answer this question with a straightforward 'yes' or 'no'. The answer will depend on which aspect of the relation between religious belief and philosophy one has in mind. It is certainly true that to philosophize is not to worship. Yet, for Socrates, to practise philosophy was to participate in a life of purification. This seems far removed from the way philosophers are regarded or regard themselves today. Yet, can no sense be given to philosophical enquiry as a form of purification?

I have now raised a difficult question, perhaps we can move some little distance towards an answer by considering a different, though related, question. In certain areas of philosophical enquiry, whatever philosophical answers we arrive at seem to have little effect on the activity we are enquiring about. For example, it seems that whatever philosophical views we hold about perception or the nature of physical objects, the way people see things, handle things, etc., goes on regardless. But is it like this where moral or religious beliefs are concerned? Can one say that, whatever answers are given in philosophy, the role which moral and religious beliefs play in people's lives goes on regardless? I do not think one can.

To begin with, we must recognize that philosophy may have had an effect already on people's religious beliefs. People need not have read any philosophy. The influence of philosophy may be direct or indirect. People's beliefs may be the product of complex sources, one of them being philosophy. Often one finds that the philosophy which has influenced people's beliefs is bad philosophy. This may lead to the loss or an obscuring of a religious understanding which might have been possible otherwise. Think, for example, of the philosophical equation of immortality and survival, eternity and duration, both of which I regard as philosophically bad. To believe that the only meaning that the immortality of the soul can have is that of survival after death, and that the only meaning eternity can have is that of infinite duration, may have various effects on one's religious beliefs. If, as a philosopher, one believes these things, one may find one's faith being destroyed, because one can see, intellectually, that it makes no sense to speak of surviving death. Because philosophy has shown the belief to be meaningless, one is forced to give it up.

But it may not have been like this. Before coming to philosophy, one may have given an account of one's belief in the immortality of the soul in terms of survival after death, but one's belief had far more to it than that. One was giving an inadequate account of what one really believed. Often, in such cases, when philosophy shows the account to be mistaken, the person concerned thinks that his faith has been shown to be mistaken too, whereas that is not the case. Religiously speaking, these occurrences are regarded as tragic. Such occurrences are the breeding-ground for religious misologists.

The influence of bad philosophy need not be destructive in the ways I have tried to describe. Bad philosophy can also be constructive, but what it creates is as confused as itself. What I mean is this: if, as a result of bad philosophy, people only give an account of the immortality of the soul in terms of survival after death, but come to believe this – that is, this is what their faith comes to be – then bad philosophy has contributed to the creation of illusions, dreams which can never be realized, and hopes which can never be fulfilled – hopes of surviving death, of meeting loved ones again, of inheriting a better life beyond the grave where the misfortunes and deprivations one has suffered in this life are compensated in full. Of course, philosophy is not the only source, and probably not even the main source, of such longings. All I am concerned to show is how philosophy can contribute to the blurring of the distinction between illusion and reality.

But this is not all. In creating such hopes, philosophy not only creates false expectations for the future, but changes the nature of one's present faith. Bad philosophy in this context makes it hard, if not impossible, to see death in any other way. The logic of death becomes akin to the logic of sleep. Once that happens, one can no longer see certain truths which death may teach. If one thinks of death, to use the words of one old Welsh divine, not as a terminus, but as a bus-stop, there is little chance of one's ever coming to understand what is meant by the majesty of death, for who would dream of talking of the majesty of sleep?

But, again, it need not have been like this. Before coming to philosophy, one may have thought of the immortality of the soul in terms of survival after death, and then come to see that one cannot speak in this way. One may come to see the possibility of speaking and thinking of the immortality of the soul in another way. Now, here, when one speaks of 'coming to understand', 'coming to see it as a possibility', 'coming to see the point of it', is it easy to draw a sharp distinction between a philosophical account of belief and believing, between giving an account of the immortality of the soul and believing in the immortality of the soul? Again, no straightforward categorical answer can be given. It may be that in an individual's experience, coming to see the point of religious beliefs is at the same time the increase or dawning of philosophical and religious understanding. What I mean is that philosophical and religious understanding go together here. The

267

deepening of philosophical understanding may at the same time be the deepening of religious understanding. The latter may be marked by the actual developments which take place in a person's faith, or in the aspirations which the new understanding creates.

Despite what I have just said, however, we cannot simply equate a philosophical understanding of religion with religious belief. For one thing, as we have seen, philosophy may obscure religious understanding – bad philosophy is still philosophy. But, more importantly, philosophical understanding of the kind I have described need not lead to a deepening of religious devotion. A person could, to some extent, come to see the kind of thing certain religious beliefs are through philosophy, and hate them all the more as a result. He may see nothing but servility in them. Or, to take a different example, a person who does not believe in God may come to see that it is possible to think about religion in a way he had been completely unaware of. Although he remains an atheist, he now sees that the ways in which he used to attack religion are nonsensical. That is all he may see. He now contents himself with saying that religion does not mean anything to him. But his life has been affected by philosophical speculation, since he can no longer think of religion as he used to.

In all the cases I have mentioned, it would be artificial to separate a person's philosophical reflections from his life. In so far as this is true, these examples stand as objections against those philosophers who speak of philosophy as a second-order activity, as something which makes no substantial difference to what is being investigated. I have endeavoured to show, by taking the death of Socrates as an example, how philosophy and what is important to one in life may be intimately bound up with one another.

I have taken the motto, *Think not of Socrates, think of the truth,* and considered it from two points of view: (*a*) from the point of view of a religious believer, (*b*) from the point of view of philosophical enquiry. I recognize that this is a distinction of convenience, since the two may overlap in a host of intricate ways. We saw that it is not true to say that religious devotion must always be justified by philosophy. We also saw how philosophical enquiry may be linked to religious understanding, and how, in any speculation on religion, philosophy cannot be divorced from the life of the enquirer.

This raises a problem which I shall just mention here. What happens when someone who is deeply religious finds himself in a situation where devotion to philosophical enquiry prevails? What are the problems which face the Christian teacher here? He may, as we have seen, give a philosophical account of religious belief which the academically weak student thinks destroys his faith, but which in fact does not. What is a teacher to do? In a university, I cannot see how he can compromise and admit intellectual dishonesty for the sake of the weak student. The problem is more acute in theological colleges, where, after all, one is training *many* kinds of priests and ministers. One does not pretend that they are meant to be philosophers, or that they will be all interested in intellectual matters. There, I do not know what the answer is. Perhaps the mistake is to look for *the* answer. All the teacher can do, probably, is to meet each problem as it arises. Such problems may arise for the university teacher too, but, harsh though it sounds, I think he must be intellectually honest and

Faith and Philosophy

admit that in this context truth is more important than
people.

References

1. *Phaedo*, 88B.
2. *Ibid.*, 90C.
3. *Ibid.*, 90D.
4. *Ibid.*, 90E.
5. *Ibid.*, 91A.
6. *Ibid.*, 91C.
7. Trans. Swenson, David F., Princeton University Press, 1946.
8. *Philosophical Fragments*, 6–7.
9. *Ibid.*, 17–18
10. *Ibid.*, 23.
11. Tolstoy, Leo., 'A Confession' in *A Confession, the Gospel in Brief
and What I believe*, trans. Maude, Aylmer, The World's Classics,
O.U.P., 1954, 5.

Bibliography

Bibliography

A: *PHILOSOPHICAL BOOKS*

ANSCOMBE, G. E. M., and GEACH, P. T., *Three Philosophers*, Blackwell, 1961.

BOUWSMA, O. K., *Philosophical Essays*, University of Nebraska Press, 1965.

CAMUS, ALBERT: *The Rebel*, trans. Bower, Anthony, Peregrine Books, 1962.

FLEW, A., and MACINTYRE, A. (eds.), *New Essays in Philosophical Theology*, S.C.M. Press, 1955.

FREUD, SIGMUND, *New Introductory Lectures on Psychoanalysis*, trans. Strachey, James, Hogarth Press, 1964.

GOLLWITZER, H. (with KUHN, K. and SCHNEIDER, R. (eds.)), *Dying We Live*, trans. Kuhn, Reinhard C., Fontana Books, 1958.

HICK, JOHN, (ed.), *Faith and the Philosophers*, London, 1964.

—— (ed.), *The Existence of God*, Macmillan, 1964.

HUME, DAVID, *Dialogues Concerning Natural Religion*, ed. Smith, Norman Kemp, The Library of Liberal Arts, Bobbs-Merrill Co., 1963.

KANT, IMMANUEL, *Fundamental Principles of the Metaphysic of Ethics*, trans. Abbott, T. K., Longmans, 1949.

KIERKEGAARD, SÖREN, *Concluding Unscientific Postscript*, trans. Swenson, David F., Princeton University Press, 1944.

—— *Works of Love*, trans. Swenson, David F. and Lillian M., O.U.P., 1946.

—— *Works of Love*, trans. Hong, Edna and Howard, Collins, 1962.

—— *Either/Or*, trans. Lowrie, Walter, O.U.P., 1946.

Bibliography

KIERKEGAARD, SÖREN, *Fear and Trembling*, trans. Payne, Robert, O.U.P., 1939.

—— *Purity of Heart*, trans. Steere, Douglas, Fontana Books, 1961.

—— *Philosophical Fragments*, trans. Swenson, David F., Princeton University Press, 1946.

LACY, ALLEN, *Miguel de Unamuno: The Rhetoric of Existence*, Mouton, 1967.

MALCOLM, NORMAN, *Knowledge and Certainty*, Prentice-Hall, 1963.

MASCALL, E. L., *Existence and Analogy*, Longmans, 1949.

MELDEN, A. I., *Rights and Right Conduct*, Blackwell, 1959.

MILL, JOHN STUART, *Utilitarianism*, ed. Warnock, Mary, Fontana Books, 1962.

MUNITZ, MILTON K., *The Mystery of Existence*, Appleton-Century-Crofts, 1965.

MUNZ, PETER, *Problems of Religious Knowledge*, S.C.M. Press, 1959.

PHILLIPS, D. Z., *The Concept of Prayer*, Routledge & Kegan Paul, 1965.

—— (ed.), *Religion and Understanding*, Blackwell, 1967.

PLATO, *Gorgias*.

—— *Phaedo*.

RAMSEY, I. T., *Models and Mystery*, O.U.P., 1964.

TOLSTOY, LEO, *A Confession, the Gospel in Brief, and What I Believe*, trans. Maude, Aylmer, O.U.P., 1954.

TOULMIN, STEPHEN, *The Place of Reason in Ethics*, C.U.P., 1950.

—— *Introduction to the Philosophy of Science*, H.U.L., 1953.

TYLOR, E. B., *Primitive Culture*, London, 1920.

WEIL, SIMONE, *Gravity and Grace*, trans. Craufurd, Emma, Routledge & Kegan Paul, 1952.

—— *Waiting on God*, trans. Craufurd, Emma, Fontana Books, 1959.

—— *The Need for Roots*, trans. Wills, A. F., Routledge & Kegan Paul, 1952.

—— *Letter to a Priest*, Routledge & Kegan Paul, 1953.

WINCH, PETER, *The Idea of a Social Science*, Routledge & Kegan Paul, 1958.

WISDOM, JOHN, *Philosophy and Psychoanalysis*, Blackwell, 1953.
—— *Paradox and Discovery*, Blackwell, 1965.

WITTGENSTEIN, LUDWIG, *Notebooks 1914–1916*, ed. Wright, G. H. von, and Anscombe, G. E. M., Blackwell, 1961.
—— *Tractatus Logico-Philosophicus*, trans. Pears, D. F., and McGuinness, B. F., Routledge & Kegan Paul, 1961.
—— *Philosophical Investigations*, trans. Anscombe, G. E. M., Blackwell, 1953.
—— *Lectures and Conversations on Aesthetics, Psychology and Religious Belief*, Blackwell, 1966.

B: *PHILOSOPHICAL PAPERS*

ANDERSON, JOHN, 'Art and Morality', *Australasian Journal of Psychology and Philosophy*, xix, 3 (December 1941).

ATKINSON, R. C., 'The Use of Models in Experimental Psychology', in *The Concept and Role of the Model in Mathematics and Natural and Social Sciences*, ed. Kazemier, B. H., and Vuysje, D., D. Reidel, Holland, 1961.

BOUWSMA, O. K., 'The Terms of Ordinary Language are . . .', in *Philosophical Essays*, University of Nebraska Press, 1965.

FLEW, A. G. N., 'Theology and Falsification', in *New Essays in Philosophical Theology*, ed. Flew, A., and MacIntyre, A., S.C.M. Press, 1955.

HEPBURN, R. W., 'From World to God', *Mind*, lxxii (1963).

HICK, JOHN, 'Sceptics and Believers', in *Faith and the Philosophers*, London, 1964.
—— 'The Justification of Religious Belief', *Theology*, lxxi (March 1968).
—— 'Theology's Central Problem', University of Birmingham, 1967.

HIRST, PAUL H., 'Morals, Religion, and the Maintained

School', *British Journal of Educational Studies*, 14 (1965–6).

JONES, J. R., 'Love as Perception of Meaning', in *Religion and Understanding*, ed. Phillips, D. Z., Blackwell, 1967.

MACINTYRE, ALISDAIR, 'The Logical Status of Religious Belief', in *Metaphysical Beliefs*, ed. MacIntyre, A., London, 1957.

—— 'Is Understanding Religion Compatible with Believing?', in *Faith and the Philosophers*, ed. Hick, John, London, 1964.

MCGUINNESS, B. F., 'The Mysticism of the *Tractatus*', *Philosophical Review*, July 1966.

MCPHERSON, T. H., 'Religion as the Inexpressible', in *New Essays in Philosophical Theology*, ed. Flew, A., and MacIntyre, A., S.C.M. Press, 1955.

MALCOLM, NORMAN, 'Anselm's Ontological Arguments', *Philosophical Review*, lxix (1960).

—— 'Is it a Religious Belief that "God Exists"?', in *Faith and the Philosophers*, ed. Hick, John, London, 1964.

NIELSEN, KAI, 'Wittgensteinian Fideism', *Philosophy* 1967.

PALMER, HUMPHREY, 'Understanding First', *Theology*, lxxi (March 1968).

PASSMORE, J. A., 'Christianity and Positivism', *Australasian Journal of Philosophy*, xxxv (1957).

POTEAT, W. H., 'Birth, Suicide, and the Doctrine of Creation: an Exploration of Analogies', *Mind*, lxviii (1959).

—— 'I Will Die', *Philosophical Quarterly*, 9 (1959).

RHEES, RUSH, 'Wittgenstein's Builders', *Proceedings of the Aristotelian Society*, 1959–60.

—— 'Some Developments in Wittgenstein's View of Ethics', *Philosophical Review*, January 1965.

SMITH, NORMAN KEMP, 'Is Divine Existence Credible?', *Proceedings of the British Academy*, 1931.

WINCH, PETER, 'Understanding a Primitive Society', *American Philosophical Quarterly*, i (1964).

WINCH, PETER, 'Can a Good Man be Harmed?', *Proceedings of the Aristotelian Society*, 1965–6.

WISDOM, JOHN, 'Gods', in *Philosophy and Psychoanalysis*, Blackwell, 1953.

—— 'The Logic of God'; 'Religious Belief'; 'Freewill'; 'Tolerance'; in *Paradox and Discovery*, Blackwell, 1965.

WITTGENSTEIN, LUDWIG, 'Lecture on Ethics', *Philosophical Review*, January 1965.